Reyes Pujol-Xicoy

# DECORATIVE WALL PAINTING

## for Beginners

**KÖNEMANN**

© 2001 Könemann Verlagsgesellschaft mbH

Bonner Straße 126 D-50968 Cologne

**Author:** Reyes Pujol-Xicoy

**Editor:** Rosa Tamarit

**Photographs:** David Manchón

**Design and Project Management:** Arco Editorial S.A

Original title: *Pintura decorativa de paredes*

© 2001 for this English edition

Könemann Verlagsgesellschaft mbH

Translation from Spanish: Maria Luengo, Stephanie Timms

Editing in association with Cambridge Publishing Management

Typesetting: Cambridge Publishing Management

Project Management: Steven Carruthers, Cambridge Publishing

Management, Cambridge, UK

Project Coordinator: Kristin Zeier

Production: Stefan Bramsiepe

Printing and Binding: Eurografica

Printed in Italy

ISBN 3-8290-6097-1

10 9 8 7 6 5 4 3 2 1

Introduction . . . . . . . . . . . . . . . . . . . . . .4

1. Materials . . . . . . . . . . . . . . . . . . . . . .6

Materials . . . . . . . . . . . . . . . . . . . . . . . . . 8
Basic materials . . . . . . . . . . . . . . . . . . . . . . . . .8
Other basic materials . . . . . . . . . . . . . . . . . . . .10
Materials needed . . . . . . . . . . . . . . . . . . . . . .10
Special brushes . . . . . . . . . . . . . . . . . . . . . . . .11
Other tools and materials . . . . . . . . . . . . . . . . .13
Pigments and colorings . . . . . . . . . . . . . . . . . .15
Water-based paints . . . . . . . . . . . . . . . . . . . . .16
Oil-based paints . . . . . . . . . . . . . . . . . . . . . . .17
Varnish . . . . . . . . . . . . . . . . . . . . . . . . . . . .18
Cleaning and maintenance . . . . . . . . . . . . . . . .19
Storing left-over paint . . . . . . . . . . . . . . . . . . .19
Step by step: Water-based glaze . . . . . . . . . . . . .20
Step by step: Oil-based glaze . . . . . . . . . . . . . .22
Step by step: Cleaning brushes . . . . . . . . . . . . .24

2. Space and color . . . . . . . . . . . . . . . . .26

1. Space . . . . . . . . . . . . . . . . . . . . . . . . . . .28
Preparing the space . . . . . . . . . . . . . . . . . . . . .28
Preparing the walls . . . . . . . . . . . . . . . . . . . . .29
2. Color . . . . . . . . . . . . . . . . . . . . . . . . . . .32
Choosing the color . . . . . . . . . . . . . . . . . . . . .32
The room . . . . . . . . . . . . . . . . . . . . . . . . . . .33
Color theory . . . . . . . . . . . . . . . . . . . . . . . .36
The color wheel . . . . . . . . . . . . . . . . . . . . . . .36

3. Step by step techniques . . . . . . . . . . .40
1. Ragging off with water-based paints . . . . . . . . . . . .42
Tips on ragging off with water-based paints . . . . . . .42
2. Ragging off with oil-based paints . . . . . . . . . . . . . .44
Tips on ragging off with oil-based paints . . . . . . . . .44

3. Dragging with water-based paints . . . . . . . . . . . . . .46

　Tips on dragging with water-based paints . . . . . . . .46

4. Sponging with two colors . . . . . . . . . . . . . . . . . . . .48

　Tips for sponging with two colors . . . . . . . . . . . . .48

5. Combing . . . . . . . . . . . . . . . . . . . . . . . . . . . . . . . .50

　Tips on combing . . . . . . . . . . . . . . . . . . . . . . . . . . .50

6. Relief combing . . . . . . . . . . . . . . . . . . . . . . . . . . . .52

　Tips on relief combing . . . . . . . . . . . . . . . . . . . . . .52

7. Stucco . . . . . . . . . . . . . . . . . . . . . . . . . . . . . . . . . .56

　Tips on stucco . . . . . . . . . . . . . . . . . . . . . . . . . . . .56

8. Rolling off . . . . . . . . . . . . . . . . . . . . . . . . . . . . . . . .60

　Tips on rolling off . . . . . . . . . . . . . . . . . . . . . . . . . .60

9. Dragging with oil-based paints . . . . . . . . . . . . . . . .62

　Tips on dragging with oil-based paints . . . . . . . . . .62

10. Raffia . . . . . . . . . . . . . . . . . . . . . . . . . . . . . . . . . . .66

　Tips on raffia . . . . . . . . . . . . . . . . . . . . . . . . . . . . . .66

11. Moiré . . . . . . . . . . . . . . . . . . . . . . . . . . . . . . . . . . .68

　Tips on moiré . . . . . . . . . . . . . . . . . . . . . . . . . . . . .68

12. Pine wood graining . . . . . . . . . . . . . . . . . . . . . . . . .70

　Tips on pine wood graining . . . . . . . . . . . . . . . . . . .70

13. Diamonds . . . . . . . . . . . . . . . . . . . . . . . . . . . . . . . .72

　Tips on diamonds . . . . . . . . . . . . . . . . . . . . . . . . . .72

14. Bricks . . . . . . . . . . . . . . . . . . . . . . . . . . . . . . . . . . .76

　Tips on bricks . . . . . . . . . . . . . . . . . . . . . . . . . . . . .76

15. Old stone wall . . . . . . . . . . . . . . . . . . . . . . . . . . . .80

　Tips on old stone wall . . . . . . . . . . . . . . . . . . . . . .80

16. Gray granite . . . . . . . . . . . . . . . . . . . . . . . . . . . . . .84

　Tips on gray granite . . . . . . . . . . . . . . . . . . . . . . . .84

17. Travertine . . . . . . . . . . . . . . . . . . . . . . . . . . . . . . . .86

　Tips on travertine . . . . . . . . . . . . . . . . . . . . . . . . . .86

18. Stenciling . . . . . . . . . . . . . . . . . . . . . . . . . . . . . . . .90

　Tips on stenciling . . . . . . . . . . . . . . . . . . . . . . . . . .90

19. Damask . . . . . . . . . . . . . . . . . . . . . . . . . . . . . . . . . .96

　Tips on damask . . . . . . . . . . . . . . . . . . . . . . . . . . . .96

20. Mosaic . . . . . . . . . . . . . . . . . . . . . . . . . . . . . . . . .100

　Tips on mosaic . . . . . . . . . . . . . . . . . . . . . . . . . . .100

21. Trellis work . . . . . . . . . . . . . . . . . . . . . . . . . . . . . .104

　Tips on trellis work . . . . . . . . . . . . . . . . . . . . . . . .104

22. Silk paper . . . . . . . . . . . . . . . . . . . . . . . . . . . . . . .110

　Tips on silk paper . . . . . . . . . . . . . . . . . . . . . . . . .110

23. Craft paper . . . . . . . . . . . . . . . . . . . . . . . . . . . . . .114

　Tips on craft paper . . . . . . . . . . . . . . . . . . . . . . . .114

24. Sgraffito . . . . . . . . . . . . . . . . . . . . . . . . . . . . . . . .120

　Tips on sgraffito . . . . . . . . . . . . . . . . . . . . . . . . . .120

25. Découpage . . . . . . . . . . . . . . . . . . . . . . . . . . . . . .122

　Tips on découpage . . . . . . . . . . . . . . . . . . . . . . . .122

26. Rust effect . . . . . . . . . . . . . . . . . . . . . . . . . . . . . .126

　Tips on rust effect . . . . . . . . . . . . . . . . . . . . . . . .126

27. Fantasy stone . . . . . . . . . . . . . . . . . . . . . . . . . . . .130

　Tips on fantasy stone . . . . . . . . . . . . . . . . . . . . . .130

28. Rustic wall . . . . . . . . . . . . . . . . . . . . . . . . . . . . . .134

　Tips on rustic wall . . . . . . . . . . . . . . . . . . . . . . . .134

29. Dry brush . . . . . . . . . . . . . . . . . . . . . . . . . . . . . . .138

　Tips on dry brush . . . . . . . . . . . . . . . . . . . . . . . . .138

30. Stone . . . . . . . . . . . . . . . . . . . . . . . . . . . . . . . . . .142

　Tips on stone . . . . . . . . . . . . . . . . . . . . . . . . . . . .142

31. Gilded garlands . . . . . . . . . . . . . . . . . . . . . . . . . . .146

　Tips on gilding garlands . . . . . . . . . . . . . . . . . . . . .146

32. Old whitewash . . . . . . . . . . . . . . . . . . . . . . . . . . .152

　Tips on old whitewash . . . . . . . . . . . . . . . . . . . . .152

33. Chalk glaze . . . . . . . . . . . . . . . . . . . . . . . . . . . . . .158

　Tips on chalk glaze . . . . . . . . . . . . . . . . . . . . . . . .158

4. Glossary . . . . . . . . . . . . . . . . . . . . . . . .164

# Introduction

Decorative paint techniques are by far the best way of transforming a room and of giving it that very personal touch. Without being a great artist you can use the simple materials and techniques described in this book to give your rooms a completely different look – to make them look cosy or spacious, elegant or rustic, familiar or exotic. Considering just how much you can change your home to suit your personal style with just a bit of paint, painted effects are one of the most economical means available. And they can also be fun!

What do you need? First, some simple, inexpensive, and easy-to-obtain tools and materials – brushes, rags, sponges etc. We will explain exactly what you need for each technique. Second, the will to give it a try. Don't feel intimidated by an untouched expanse of white wall – if you don't like what you've done, you only have to

paint over it and regard the time used as an opportunity to practice and experiment. This book is intended to be both a guide to techniques and a spur to your creativity.

We will list the materials and tools you'll need and explain how to use them efficiently. We will offer professional tips and advice that will make the tasks easier and more pleasant, and we will guide you in the choice of the colors that will both express your personality and also suit the character of the rooms themselves. And we will explain all this in a very simple and practical way, step by step.

## What are decorative paint techniques?

When we try to define decorative painted effects (it seems natural to distinguish them from 'art painting'), we get into a very tricky area – we need criteria to differentiate Art with a capital A from all that is generally called craft.

# Where is the dividing line?

In many of our museums there are wonderful murals that in their time were created for a purely decorative purpose, such as those of Pompeii and Knossos – yet to many contemporary artists the word 'decorative' is demeaning.

Those who have cultivated an interest in both aspects of painting, as I have, realize that in reality this dividing line is not at all clear. Any idea that we want to express on a canvas will require materials and techniques similar to those used to decorate a wall. Equally, in any decorated wall we will find clear evidence of the sensitivity, taste, and personality of its creator – which in Art they might call 'the spirit of the artist.'

Perhaps the difference lies in their basic aims. It is obvious that mural painting is used primarily (but not exclusively) to protect surfaces from the elements and from wear and tear. Of humble origins, it was long subordinate to architecture, and often did not aspire to go any further. But though it may not always be something created for itself, as an independent work, decorative painting *is* a means of humanizing our surroundings – and this is as true for the man who left his handprints in a prehistoric cave as for those who, in reading this book, are planning to decorate their home, whether a grand house or a modest apartment.

In both cases a desire takes form – to express one's individuality, to leave the mark of one's personality in a space that may otherwise have remained dull and lifeless. Decorative paint techniques allow us to modify our habitats and adapt them to our personality. They are a simple way of making our life more pleasant, and at the same time an excellent excuse for all those people who have always felt intimidated by Art but who now can pick up a brush, dab it in bright paint, and give free reign to their imagination.

*Reyes Pujol-Xicoy*

1.Materials

# I. Materials

Many of the materials needed for the decorative paint techniques described in this book are the same as those used in conventional house painting: paint brushes of different sizes and shapes, rollers, sandpaper, water-based paint, putty, a palette knife to repair cracks, a plastic trowel, etc. You may already have most of these tools and materials; if not, you can easily find them in any hardware or Do It Yourself (DIY) store.

To achieve some of the painted effects we describe, you may also need other common materials, such as sponges, feathers, rags, or paper – these are used to create different finishes and textures.

Only on a few occasions should it be necessary to go to specialist art shops for very fine brushes or specific tools, such as badger-hair brushes, graining rockers, or combs (all these terms will be explained as we go along).

Many people think that these special tools can be improvised; they can, but frankly you won't get the same results.

## Basic materials:

### Paintbrushes

Quality paintbrushes have handles made of hard wood protected by a resistant varnish, and bristles that are firmly held in place by a metal rust-resistant band called a ferrule.

Some brushes are round and have a crown-shaped arrangement of bristles; these are classified according to their diameter, which is usually written on the ferrule or on the handle. Brushes with a flat section are classified according to their width. Flat brushes, one of the most versatile tools in home decorating, are used to paint the base coat before the decorative paint techniques are applied, and then to cover the wall with varnish after the decorative effects have been created.

## Rollers

Recently rollers have became very popular as an alternative to brushes, and there are now rollers for a range of different purposes. They are particularly useful for applying the base coat to large surfaces as they give a regular and uniform finish, and they are relatively easy and quick to use.

Rollers usually consist of an interchangeable cylindrical sleeve attached to a handle. The sleeves can be of different materials and sizes. For water-based paints, sheepskin sleeves are the best as they hold a good deal of paint without dripping. For oil-based paints, use rollers with short fibers.

Rollers are used with a ribbed tray that helps to remove excess paint. Rollers with detachable extension handles are ideal for painting high surfaces.

To start with you will need only four flat brushes of different sizes: 100 mm (4 in.), 50 mm (2 in.), 25 mm (1 in.), and 13 mm ($^1/_2$ in.). You can buy other special brushes as and when you need them. If you plan to work with water-based paints as well as oil-based paints, it is advisable to have separate brushes for each kind of paint.

Flat brushes commonly used in decoration often lose some bristles when new. To get rid of loose bristles, slap the brush vigorously back and forth against the palm of your hand before using it. Then soften the bristles by soaking them in a jar of water for a day; make sure that the bristles are not touching the bottom of the jar, or they may become misshapen.

Always buy good quality brushes. If you take the trouble to clean them properly after use, they will last you many years and the results will be much more professional – cheap brushes usually lose bristles and leave marks that can be hard to eradicate.

## Other basic materials

To repair cracks and holes in the wall, you will need filler (in powder or ready-to-use form), a palette knife, and sandpaper.

There are different grades of sandpaper, most commonly numbered according to the size of the grain. The lower numbers represent the coarser grain, and the higher numbers the finer grain. This number is usually printed on the back of the paper.

There are also sandpapers that can be used wet to give a very fine finish; they also avoid the inconvenience of dust. They are the most suitable for use on varnish, while the dry ones are best for smoothing down any roughness on dry walls.

Finally, the strength of sandpapers can vary. Only those with a strong and flexible support can be used with an electric sander without breaking up. To use sandpaper manually, wrap it around a block of wood that you can easily hold in your hand, and rub it over the surface as if you were using a blackboard eraser. There is also a new type of easy-to-use sanding sponge available – in fine, medium, and coarse grain – that can be used in the same way.

Other useful materials include: masking tape (available in different widths), rubber gloves, paper masks (for dust and fumes), rags, news-paper or plastic sheets to cover furniture, jars of different sizes, screw drivers, pliers, and a good stable ladder.

Sometimes a level may be needed to form a straight line.

## Materials needed

As well as sharing some tools and materials with conventional house painting, decorative techniques require some specific tools of their own. Some materials, used to create certain special effects, have found their way into the toolbox of the decorative painter as a result of experimenting with different techniques; others have been specially designed for a particular purpose.

# Special brushes

Brushes vary both in size and in the material from which they are made (usually animal hair). Their arrangement and length can also vary, and so can the shape of the ferrule (flat or round). This great diversity makes possible the infinite range of effects and textures that can be created.

There is also of course a practical aspect: you would not paint small details with a large brush, nor paint a large surface with a thin brush.

It is important to use each brush for the particular purpose it was designed for, ensuring that it is the right size, shape, and material for the job.

## Pure badger-hair softener

Made from genuine badger hair, this brush is very soft and so can be used, for example, to blur the veins in marbling. Badger-hair brushes are expensive and so must be cleaned carefully.

## Hog-hair softener

A very versatile tool, the hog-hair softener is wide and made with short bristles. It is used to blur work done with oil-based paints and for techniques such as colorwash.

## Pure bristle flogger

This is a straight brush with very long thick bristles and a wooden handle. It is used by slapping the bristles against a wet surface to create the flecked appearance of wood, or alternatively a characteristic striped effect.

## Pencil overgrainer

This consists of a row of fine brushes. It is used to simulate the veining of wood and for other special effects, such as raffia.

## Mottlers

Mottlers have wide rather than long handles, and can be straight or wavy. You can reproduce the characteristic graining found in maple and mahogany, by making a slight zigzag movement as you draw the mottler across a surface.

## Stippling brush

A stippling brush looks like a broom, with the bristles cut to exactly the same length. It is always held perpendicular to the surface. The brush is dabbed over a surface with a uniform pressure to produce a mottling effect that often 'ages' a surface.

## Stencil brushes

Stencil brushes have a short handle and thick bristles all cut to the same length. You apply the paint to a stencil by making circular or dabbing movements with the stencil brush.

## Slant brush

With its bristles cut to form a slant, this brush is useful for drawing fine lines, shadows, and for painting moldings.

## Thin brushes

Thin brushes are used to paint details. The best are made of sable, though cheaper ones made of other animal hair can also be used.

## Fan brushes

A very delicate brush, with bristles arranged in a fan shape. It is used to blur small details and to create characteristic veining.

## Check graining roller

This form of roller consists of a row of indented discs that rotate freely as the roller is drawn over a surface, creating a pattern that resembles the grain of certain woods.

# Other tools and materials

## Spatter brush

This brush has long, tough, rubber bristles, and is the only brush that doesn't make contact with the painted surface. It is loaded with paint that is flicked off as drops or splashes. It is very useful in reproducing the dotted look of some stones and marbles

## Graining rocker

These tools are available in two widths, 75 and 125 mm (3in. and 5in.). They are used for simulating the knots found in wood by rocking the grainer as you slide it along. Without this rocking movement only straight grains would be produced.

## Pencil overgrainer without handle

This brush, made from a row of separate bunches of bristles, is used to reproduce wood grains.

## Graining combs

These combs, made of flexible steel, have square, parallel teeth. The combs with thicker teeth are used to reproduce the thick and straight grains characteristic of certain woods. Those with thinner teeth are used to interrupt the graining. Combs can also be used to create a slight relief on paint which is not quite dry.

## Feathers

Feathers are an alternative to fine watercolor brushes, and are used to imitate marble; feathers produce random lines similar to the natural veining of some marbles.

## Sponges

Natural sponges are the best: synthetic ones are very rigid and have a very regular shape and texture. A good tip is to use large sponge to cover surfaces quickly, and small sponges to get into the corners.

## Rags

Some techniques utilize the marks left by rubbing cotton rags or gauze over wet paint.

It is a good idea to always have some rags handy. Even if you are not planning to do any ragging (a technique that will be explained later), you will find that they are useful for wiping up splashes, wiping your hands, cleaning tools, and drying brushes.

For some techniques, such as ragging and flogging, you can use tools and materials other than those we mention. This can produce interesting results that will be very different to those you will get by following our instructions to the letter. Try experimenting with everyday objects and materials, such as pan scourers, kitchen paper, plastic bags, or anything else you can think of.

Sometimes the same effect can be achieved by using different tools and techniques, for example the veining of marble can be produced using a feather or a brush.

## Paints

Some age-old paint formulas – using egg-yolk, casein (a milk by-product), or rabbit-skin glue – are still in use. Side by side with these are modern ones with a base of synthetic resin.

Together with solvents (water in this case), pigments and binder, there are also 'enhancers' such as kaolin, mica, or talc that improve adhesion, opacity, and resistance to cracking. Above all, enhancers add bulk, replacing some of the pigment and resins and reducing the cost of the paint.

Be wary of using cheap products. It is very likely that cheap paint will contain reduced amounts of pigment and this will make it difficult to achieve the effect of saturated color (another term that will be explained shortly).

### Glazes

Glazes are a semitransparent medium of light viscosity and of a slow drying time. Because they are tinted, they will modify the color of the base over which they are painted. Ensure that the drying time leaves you with ample opportunity to create the decorative effects you have chosen.

Glazes have been used for centuries in artistic paintings. Applied over a properly prepared base, they give unequalled transparency and purity of color. They also give a surface a sense of depth.

Because it's necessary to dilute the paint a great deal to produce the glaze, the color will be much lighter when it dries. It isn't possible to anticipate accurately the degree to which this will happen, so it is advisable to dye the paints with universal stainers or powder pigments that allow you to continue adding color as you work in order to get the desired result.

## Pigments and colorings

Soluble colorings (stainers) and powder pigments can be used to dye both water-based or oil-based paints. But you will probably notice a slight difference between the two kinds of paint due to the chemical properties of the colorings. Liquid colorings are completely soluble in water and oil and so leave no trace or sediment.

Powder pigment, by contrast, even though it is finely ground, is not necessarily a soluble substance – the solid particles of the pigment disperse in the water or the oil but they never quite dissolve. Depending on the size of the particles, you will probably find visible traces of pigment granules that will be randomly distributed over the surface of a painted area.

# Water-based paints

Most of the techniques explained in this book are carried out using water-based paint, so that they will be soluble in water. Water-based paint is very popular because it is easy to work with, it does not give off a toxic or unpleasant odor, and the brushes and other tools used with it are easy to clean. It also has the advantage of being cheaper and more ecologically friendly.

Water-based paint has a high covering potential, which means that you can cover a dark wall with a lighter color. The colors given by good quality water-based paint do not fade and white never turns yellowish. On the other hand they dry quickly, which is fine for most techniques but is a problem when a technique requires a long time; in this case you will need to add a retardant to the paint.

The final result is a porous, very pleasant matt look, suitable for rustic or natural settings.

## Base coat
For water-based paint effects use a base coat of soft-sheen emulsion paint. The wall should be sealed properly and should be smooth and slippery so that it is easy to apply the paint.

Remember that you cannot apply water-based paint to an oil-based surface because it will not adhere properly. Although it is rare to find walls covered with oil-based paint, if you do, they will have to be sanded down and covered with an acrylic-based paint before any emulsion can be applied.

To tell whether a surface is painted with an oil- or with a water-based paint, take some cotton wool, soak it alcohol, and rub it over a small area of paint. If it is water-based, the cotton wool will be sticky and stained with paint; if it is oil-based, the cotton wool will remain clean.

## Glaze
The ingredients required to make a water-based glaze are:

• 4 parts of water

• 1 part of latex

• 1 part of white vinyl silk emulsion paint

Make sure you prepare enough to cover the surface to be treated. Half a liter of water-based glaze will cover an area of approximately 20 square meters (210 square feet).

The result of mixing these three ingredients is a glaze similar to commercial ones, but without the added pigments. It can be stored and dyed whenever you need it. Close the jar tightly to prevent the glaze from drying.

In our sample, we will create a glaze using French Ultramarine blue pigment a blue typical of the Mediterranean.

Universal stainers, gouache, or acrylic paints can also be used – but never oil paints.

## Oil-based paints

Most oil-based paints use raw linseed oil as a medium. Once this oil is dry, it forms a layer that gets gradually harder with the years and so forms a surface resistant to solvents and cleaning products. In other words, this base is ideal when looking for lasting finishes that will be completely waterproof and repel dirt – in other words it's ideal for kitchens and bathrooms.

Walls painted with oil-based paints have a bright, sumptuous finish, the colors having an unequalled saturation and transparency. Because of its slow drying time (around 12 hours, depending on the humidity, the condition of the wall, and the thickness of the coat) oil-based

paint is very suitable for the most time-consuming techniques, such as the grain in wood and the veining in marble.

The disadvantages of oil-based paints are its high cost, the strong smell, and the tendency to yellow with heat and light. Above all you need to pay special attention to blue shades: as the colors yellow, the blues in particular will tend to come out looking duller and darker than you might have expected.

### Base coat

To use oil-based techniques apply a base coat of satin oil-based paint or of vinyl silk emulsion paint, because oil-based paint will adhere without difficulty to emulsion paint.

If the wall to be treated has already been painted matt, you should apply a coat of latex or acrylic varnish before applying the glaze. This will give a waterproof finish to the base coat.

# Varnish

It is not strictly necessary to apply varnish to a wall painted with oil-based paint, as the paint itself will give a shine to the surface. Also, when the linseed oil has hardened, it will have formed a very resistant, hard-wearing, and completely washable surface. It is only necessary to varnish an oil-painted wall if it is going to be subjected to a great deal of wear and tear.

It is a good idea to apply a final coat of varnish to walls covered with water-based paints, however, because they are more vulnerable to picking up dirt. Varnish also gives a more finished look and can enhance the decorative effect.

The most commonly used varnishes for walls are acrylic, synthetic, and polyurethane.

Acrylic varnishes are suitable only for water-based paints with a matt or gloss finish. They are not as resistant as the oil-based varnishes and though they do not yellow with time, they form a slightly blue coat over the darker colors.

Synthetic and polyurethane varnishes, which are soluble in white spirit, are harder than the acrylic varnishes. They are washable and can be applied over any surface.

Synthetic varnishes are best for giving a decorative finish to a wall. They can be matt, satin or gloss, and help to protect the surface from damage.

The choice between a gloss, satin or matt finish will also depend on your preference for the final effect.

In general, a matt finish is more suitable for rustic effects. But you have to remember that although matt varnish is durable, it doesn't protect the surface from grease, so it is not suitable for use in a kitchen.

Gloss varnish is extremely resistant and easy to clean, but it reflects light brightly so it can be undesirable in certain lighting conditions. It can also emphasize irregularities on the wall. Gloss varnish should be applied on a dry and dust-free surface, with a clean, good quality brush that has long, soft bristles.

The drying time is usually indicated on the container. Synthetic varnish and polyurethane dry in 6 to 8 hours, which means that a second coat can be applied the next day. To get a very smooth and professional finish, sand the surface with wet sanding paper.

## Cleaning and maintenance

If you clean your tools carefully, you won't have to replace them and they will be ready for use the next time you need them. When brushes have a residue of dry paint they are unable to spread paint properly, and leave irreparable marks. So stop painting half an hour before the end of your working day and spend the time cleaning your tools and brushes thoroughly.

The cleaning process varies depending on the kind of paint used. Oil-based paint requires solvents such as white spirit. Brushes that have been used for water-based paint are cleaned using just soap and water. When you work with latex it is very important to clean the brushes *immediately* after use.

## Storing left-over paint

Make sure that the tin is the right size for the amount of paint left over. Keeping a small amount of paint in a big tin encloses too much air; the paint will absorb the air and harden rapidly. To seal the tin, place a block of wood over the lid and hit it with a hammer until the lid fits perfectly. Store the tins upside-down in a cool, dry place.

It is also a good idea to write clearly on the tins the kind of paint it is, where it was used, and any other information that you think will be useful. The day you need to do some retouching, you'll be glad you did this!

# Step by step

# Water-based glaze

In this case, we will add ultramarine blue pigment directly to the glaze, a blue so typical of the Mediterranean.

Universal stainers, water-based paints, or acrylic paints can also be used, but never oil paints.

**Materials:**
- *pigment*
- *4 parts of water*
- *1 part of latex*
- *1 part of soft-sheen white paint*

## Tips

If the glaze is too thick or opaque, it can be thinned with water. If, on the other hand, it drips freely, more latex or paint should be added.

Don't use up the ingredients completely when preparing the glaze, because you may need to adjust the proportions.

*Select a bowl that is the right size for the amount of glaze you want to prepare, and put in 4 parts of water.*

Add the pigment and mix well. Keep testing as you add pigment until you get the color you want. Not all pigments have the same coloring power. A smaller amount will give a more transparent result.

Next add 1 part of latex. This binding substance, which is elastic and very adhesive, forms a light film that gives resistance against light and aging.

Stir the mix properly. If you use the right amount, the glaze should adhere firmly and allow the color of the base coat to shine through.

Finally, add 1 part of white soft-sheen emulsion paint.

# Step by step

You'll need the following:

- 1 part of raw linseed oil

- 2 parts of white spirit or solvent

- 1 part of matt, satin, or gloss varnish according to the final look you want to achieve.

**Materials:**
- white spirit
- artists' oil paint or powder pigment

## Tip

Take great care when using ingredients for the oil-based glaze as they are inflammable: it's a good idea to throw all used rags into a bucket of water – and of course don't smoke!

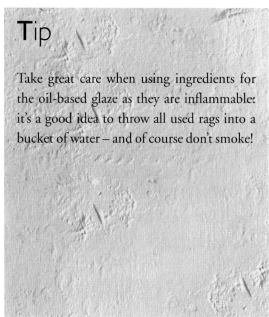

It's handy to prepare some glaze with no color, and store it so it will be ready to use when you need it. Make sure the jar is closed tightly.

 **1**

*Put the paint in a bowl. In our example we'll use burnt sienna artists' oil color.*

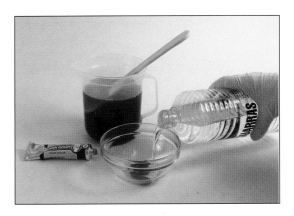

 **2**

*Pour a bit of solvent or white spirit onto the paint.*

 **3**

*Stir the mixture properly until the color has dissolved. (The same applies if you use powder pigment.)*

 **4**

*Now add the glaze you prepared earlier to get a burnt sienna glaze.*

# Step by step

Stains and putty remains can easily be cleaned wet. If incrustations have formed on the palette knives, use another palette knife or scraper to remove the larger bits and then sand down the surface with fine sandpaper.

Remember, it's a good idea to clean the containers that you wish to use, such as the roller tray.

 **1**

*Wring the brush dry and wipe it with kitchen paper or an old rag to get rid of as much paint as possible.*

## Tip

If you're thinking of stopping work for a short while, you can wrap your bushes in foil or a plastic bag until you start working again. You can immerse brushes used with oil-based paint in a jar of white spirit. To make sure the bristles don't touch the bottom, pass a wire through the hole in the handle and suspend the brush from the top of the jar.

 **2**

*If oil-based paint or glaze has been used, then use white spirit or solvent. If emulsion paint was used, plenty of warm water will do the job.*

 **3**

Next, to remove the rest of the paint, whether oil-based or water-based, put a few drops of washing-up liquid on the bristles.

 **4**

Rub the flat brush on a rough surface to work the soap into the roots of the bristles, which is where the paint tends to dry the hardest.

 **5**

Rinse thoroughly under a faucet to remove the soap.

 **6**

Hang the brush in a well-aired room with the bristles facing down. Do not put the brushes away until they are completely dry, otherwise they tend to go moldy.

# 2. Space and color

# I. Space

## Preparing the space

### Before starting

The easiest and most comfortable way of working in a room is to empty it of all furniture. You'll avoid staining them with paint, tripping over them, and suffering the discomfort of having to work in a cluttered space. Any furniture left in the room should of course be covered with sheets of polythene or cloth. Wrap the radiators and any other fittings with polythene, newspapers, or masking tape.

### Walls

Remove any wall lamps or other decorative fittings that could make your task more difficult, for example curtain poles, shelves, etc. Don't forget to make safe any electrical connections this may expose. Cover the edges of the electrical switches carefully using masking tape. Although some models of switches have frames that are easily detached, don't take the risk of removing them unless you really know what you are doing. Don't forget to extract all the nails, hooks, and cable clips that may have been left on the wall.

### Protecting edges

The easiest way to protect door and window frames is to use a wide masking tape; ceilings and the skirting boards can be protected in the same way. Pay special attention when covering corners, and remember to leave the tape in place until the paint is completely dry.

Finally, cover the floor with newspapers or a large sheet of polythene.

It's a good idea to get a long spirit level. It will allow you to draw a level horizontal line between what needs to be painted and what does not. Then apply masking tape, carefully following the line you've drawn – it's easy for the tape to gradually move away from a line.

Remember, brush strokes made at an acute angle to the masking tape may cause some paint to seep under the edges, especially if you are using a very loaded brush or the paint is very runny. To prevent this, take the precaution of stroking the brush away from the masking tape.

*This would be the appearance of the room after covering up the defects on the walls.*

## Preparing the walls

Decorative paint techniques can greatly improve the look of your room, but let's not kid ourselves, the small defects that may lie underneath will not disappear; it may even be more visible afterwards. So it's not advisable to skip a careful preparation of wall surfaces.

In most cases, you'll find that the walls have only a little damage, usually thin cracks or small holes; preparing these walls for painting is a quick and easy task. If, however, you find damp patches or cracks due to structural movement, you should consult a professional.

### Cleaning the surface

Inspect the wall carefully: if it's dirty or has any greasy patches, first remove the dust with a cloth or vacuum cleaner and then wash the dirt or grease away with soapy water. Ordinary washing-up liquid works well.

Ventilate the room so that the wall is able to dry thoroughly. Next, look for any peeling paper or paint, nail holes, cracks and any other imperfections, marking them with adhesive tape (it's very easy to forget some little hole here and there) and then repair them according to the following instructions.

### Peeling paint

Using a palette knife, scrape away any paint that isn't firmly stuck to the wall. The unevenness that results is easily eliminated by sanding or by the use of filler, which is applied with a wide palette knife and then sanded when dry.

### Cracks

Use a screwdriver or the edge of a palette knife to widen the cracks – this will help the filler to stay in place. After cleaning away the dust and grit, wet the crack with a brush and then force the filler deep inside.

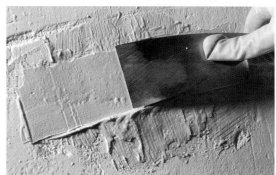

It's better to fill the cracks and holes little by little, waiting for each amount to dry before applying the next layer – if you put too much in at once it can overflow or simply come out in a lump when dry.

Once the filler is quite dry, sand until the surface is completely smooth. If it's a very large area, then you can use an electric sander. Alternatively, use sandpaper wrapped around a block of wood or cork.

If you are trying to fill a small crack and don't want to sand it, fill the gap until it overflows slightly. After five minutes – when the filler has started to dry – wipe a damp cloth over it until it's smooth. There are different kinds of commercial filler or plaster for different uses (exteriors, cracks that move, general use for interiors) and they come in powder form (which you have to make up) or ready to use. Whichever form you

form you use, always buy a good quality filler; it saves time and money in the long run.

## Applying the base coat

Once the wall is smooth and clean, it will be necessary to apply one or two coats of paint to form the base coat; make sure the first coat is dry before applying the second one. The base coat can be applied with a brush or a roller. The roller is quick and easy but will use more paint.

In both cases, start by painting the corners and the edges of the wall first, where you have applied masking tape. Do this with a 50 mm (2 in.) brush. It's important to apply the right amount of paint: not too thick and not too thin. Next, apply brush strokes on top of these and parallel to the masking tape. It is advisable to start by painting the top corners and then to work 'away and down'.

If you are going to paint the ceiling as well, do this first.

## With paintbrush

Pour part of your paint into a can. Dip half of the brush into the paint and wipe the excess paint off on the inside of the can. To paint a big area, it's advisable to do it methodically by dividing it into sections that can be covered easily without you needing to move, e.g. 60 cm × 90 cm (2 feet by 3 feet). Hold the brush at a 45° angle and paint a marked area horizontally, without applying great pressure. Next, to eliminate the horizontal lines that the bristles may have left, brush across them with the brush nearly empty. When painting the top of the wall brush towards the bottom, and towards the top when painting the bottom half of the wall.

Ensure that you blend adjacent areas thoroughly *before* the paint dries.

## With roller

Pour paint onto the tray, dip the roller in up to a third of its depth, and then roll it over the ribs – this both removes excess paint and spreads it evenly around the roller. Run the roller over the wall in all directions, making sure that it rolls and doesn't slide.

# 2. Color

 Fig. 1

*In this room the ceiling looks closer because light, warm colors have been used. At the same time, the wall has a feeling of depth because it has been covered with a blue glaze.*

When you decide to paint a room, the very first thing to consider, and long before you start the immediate preparations, is color.

## Choosing the color

The choice of colors depends on a number of things, including fashion, personal preference, and the room's function. You will also have to consider such factors as how light you want the room to be, the quality of its natural and artificial light, and the sheen of its surfaces.

### Light

One of the first things to remember is that your choice of colors will determine in general terms how dark or light the room will be – it's very easy to create a room that is far darker than you expected. So it's a good idea to study the space you are going to paint and then try a few simple experiments. For example, try a very light or pastel color, and don't be shy about experimenting with yellows, blues, ochres, etc. The small commercial sample cards of tints may not always be a sure guide. To try a color more effectively, paint it directly onto the wall and leave it to dry. Cover enough to enable you to imagine the final result; place some furniture or a carpet near the painted patch to see how the color combination works. If you don't want to paint the wall itself, paint a large sheet of cardboard and put that against the wall.

## Quality of light

The amount of light in a room and its source should always be kept in mind when planning your color scheme. This is not just a question of whether a room is well or poorly lit; it's important to remember that color itself is largely determined by the light that illuminates it. Moreover, the effect the light has will depend on whether it is natural light, artificial light, or a mixture of both.

## Surface sheen

Besides the color itself, the finish of the surfaces – matt, satin, or gloss – are important. The finish will make the light in the room reflect in different ways and so produce very different kinds of illumination.

 Fig. 2

*In this bathroom the use of similar colors for the walls and the ceiling has enhanced the sense of space.*

# The room

In general, softer pastel colors, particularly in cold tones, will make the walls seem farther away, while warmer, brighter colors will make them feel closer. The addition of glaze to a light base coat will enhance the impression of spaciousness. Unlike the more familiar forms of painting, glazing increases the sense of depth because light passes through a glaze and is then reflected back from the base color – the light seems to come from behind the glaze.

## Small spaces

The best ways of making a room look bigger are: (a) choose light colors, and (b) use the same color for walls and ceiling so as to avoid emphasising the differences between surfaces (see Fig. 2). It is certainly not advisable to create strong contrasts. If the ceiling is low, paint it white or use a color that is lighter that the one used on the walls. This will also make the room brighter.

 *Fig. 3*

*In this room, which has the very distinctive style of a spacious colonial residence, warm and contrasting colors have been used.*

## Large spaces

Many people would like to have this problem! In fact, an excessively large room can easily appear cold and inhospitable. If this is your problem, warm bright colors (saturated yellows, oranges, and brownish reds) will make the room seems much cosier.

If the ceiling is very high, paint it in a similar but darker shade than the one used for the walls. If you want to make a high ceiling look lower, but you also want to keep it light in color (for instance you may want it to reflect light), the solution is to give more visual weight to the walls by painting a horizontal stripe around them in a contrasting color.

## The room

Are you going to paint a hall or a kitchen? Is it a child's room or an office? Although the only restrictions on the choice of colors are the ones we impose on ourselves, there are a few things that you may want to consider regarding the function of the room that is going to be painted.

Is it an area you simply pass through, or a place where you are going to spend many hours? Who will be using it, and what will it be used for?

The most common disadvantage of passing-through spaces like halls and corridors is that they can be narrow and dark. Their advantage, by contrast, is that they allow us to make a strong impression through the use of unusual techniques and very daring colors – as we are not going to stay in them long, we won't feel oppressed by them however daring they are.

A living room should generally have a more relaxing feel, as should bedrooms and studies. This doesn't mean that bright colors can't be used in such rooms, but bear in mind that they can be tiring on the eyes, or have a negative effect on your state of mind. Although we are not generally conscious of it, it seems that color affects our nervous system and can subliminally modify how we think and feel.

Red is an exciting color, capable (apparently) of increasing the heart beat; culturally it is associated with passion, which would explain its use in discotheques. Blues and greens are believed to increase concentration at work; yellows and

Fig. 4 and 5

*Choosing the right colors for the walls can transform and personalize a space.*

oranges inject vitality, purples help balance the mind… and so on.

These principles are of course based on general experience – it's rare to find an environment in which the colors are completely pure or sufficiently isolated to test this theory in detail; and besides, the effects colors have are strongly influenced by a range of cultural factors. Nevertheless, it is helpful to keep a few basic principles about 'color and mood' in mind as you choose colors – colors that must not only suit your personality, but also create an effect appropriate to a room's use.

## Style

The most important factor in determining the style and character of a house or apartment is, without doubt, the personality of those who live in it.

In contrast to the uniformity of a block of apartments, each individual apartment can have its own distinctive and unique character – there is no single formula that is valid for everyone when it comes to color and decoration.

Color is so crucial in determining the style of a home that it is essential that you first clearly define what style you want, and then decide on the colors you will need to create it. You can choose warm and classic Mediterranean colors, Scandinavian blue-grays and whites to get a more relaxing and natural atmosphere, neutral colors, sober and elegant colors, strong Mexican colors, pastels from the 1930s... and all those you can improvise according to your own taste.

## Color theory

If you have never experimented with colors, it would be a good idea to have five jars of tempera or gouache next to you as you read this chapter. You can learn a great deal from a few simple experiments.

The only *pigment* colors that you will need to obtain any color you like are: yellow, magenta, cyan, white, and black. The first three are called primary colors. By combining them, any tint or hue can be obtained. Adding white will make the color lighter, and black will darken it.

## The color wheel

The color wheel (or chromatic circle) represents the relationships between the colors of the spectrum in a clear and diagrammatic way; it is particularly useful in showing what shade is produced when two colors are mixed.

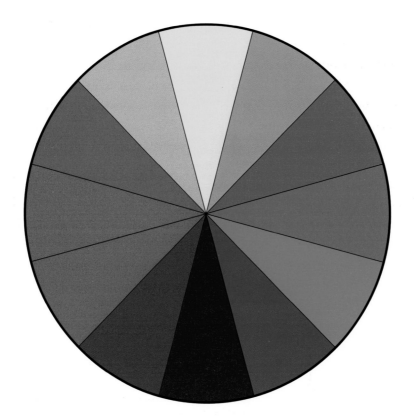

 Fig. 6

*The color wheel used by decorators is based on the systematic combination of the three primary colors: red (magenta), yellow, and blue (cyan).*

The color wheel is divided into six or twelve equal parts: opposite one another are the three *primary* colors. Half way between them are the *secondary* colors: these are obtained by mixing primary colors in equal amounts: orange, from mixing yellow and magenta; green, from yellow and cyan, and violet, from magenta and cyan.

With a further subdivision we get the *tertiary* colors; these are the result of mixing a primary color and an adjacent secondary color in equal amounts. For instance, from the mixture of magenta and violet, we get purple. Tertiary colors can be mixed with each other to produce an infinite variety of shades.

Opposite colors in the color wheel are called *complementary*. So, yellow, which is a primary color, has violet as a complementary. A color mixed in equal quantity with its complementary, produces gray. Adding only small amounts of a complementary and adjusting it with white, will give the neutral colors that are so fashionable at the moment. A blue hue, for instance, turns towards gray when you add orange.

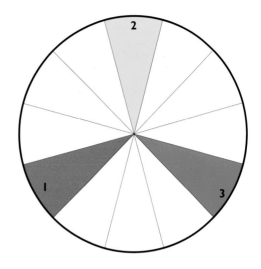

 Fig. 7

The position of the three primary colors within the color wheel: red (magenta) (1); yellow (2); and blue (cyan) (3).

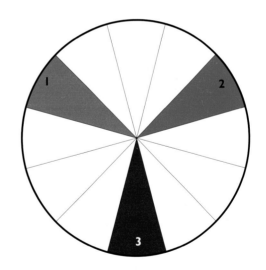

 Fig. 8

The position of the three secondary colors within the color wheel: orange (1), green (2), and violet (3).

*Value* or *tone* is the lightness or darkness of a color. It has nothing to with the hue, so a green and a red may have the same value and, as a consequence, appear very similar in a black and white photograph. In terms of value, colors are referred to as light or dark.

*Chrome* is the proportion of pure pigment that the colors contain. Colloquially we would talk of a strong or saturated color.

*Shades* are the colors produced by combining with other colors; this is what allows us to talk about blue-greens, turquoise, orange-reds, etc.

*Pastel* colors are obtained by adding large amounts of white to a color.

## Mixing colors

Once you have a clear idea of the color you want, you can use various methods to produce it. The most common method is to mix pigments into the paint until you get the precise color you are searching for. But there is no reason why you shouldn't resort to existing colors as a base, especially if you want a very saturated color (creating saturated colors requires a great deal of pigment). As work proceeds, you may of course have to adjust your color slightly by the judicious use of pigments.

## Vocabulary of color

*Hue* is what tells one color apart from another – such as red from green. With paint, the hue is determined by the pigment. In terms of physics, colors are wavelengths of light that objects either reflect or absorb; if an object reflects a red wave length of light but absorbs all the others, we see that object as red. White does not absorb any wavelengths and reflects all light; black absorbs all the light and reflects none.

*Neutral* colors are obtained by mixing a base color with a small amount of its complementary color and some white; the result is a delicately tinted gray.

## Color combination

In an interior, colors do not exist in isolation but in relation to one another, each modifying the intrinsic properties of the others. You should try to anticipate how the hue, value, and chrome of a color will be affected by those of the colors around it. To do this you will also need to consider the furniture, woodwork, surrounding walls, curtains or rugs that will be adjacent to each wall.

Remember that the success of decoration does not lie simply in the *choice* of colors – but in the *balance* between them. Combinations of color are made according to two basic principles: contrast and harmony.

# 3. Step by step techniques

# Step by step     1. Ragging off (water-based)

Water-based paint is widely used to decorate walls because it gives results that are difficult to obtain by other means.

    This technique, when used with a range of sienna colors, gives a classic and much sought-after finish.

**Materials:**
- *white soft-sheen emulsion paint*
- *latex/acrylic medium*
- *ultramarine blue pigment*
- *water*
- *cotton rags*

## Tip

Correct ragging gives a soft texture; the more crumpled the rag the softer the texture. The final look will depend on the base color and glaze, but the result can be intensified if necessary by applying a second glaze over a dry area and repeating the process. The task is much easier if you work with another person. While one person applies the glaze, the other can rag the wet wall uninterrupted. This way it is not necessary to work in discrete areas and the result is quite even.

 1

*Prepare the water-based glaze using the above ingredients, as described in chapter one. The result should have a milky appearance and a blue color (the shade will of course depend on the amount of pigment used).*

 **2**

Apply random brushstrokes of glaze over the color base emulsion paint, using a flat brush. The quick drying time of water-based glaze will not allow you to work with large areas, so work on an area of say one square meter (10 square feet) at a time.

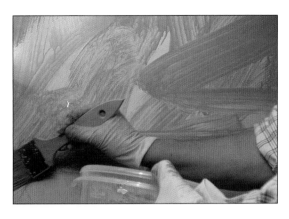

 **3**

Cover the background completely, leaving irregular edges that will be easier to blend with the area to be painted next.

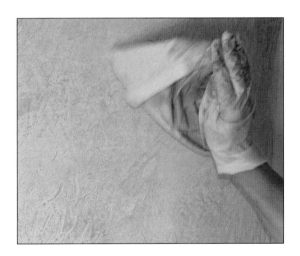

 **4**

Dab the glaze with a crumpled rag. Refold it as it gets soaked and have a few more handy so you can change them. No visible brush strokes should be left. When you are happy with the result in one area, apply the glaze on the adjacent area and proceed with the ragging. Pay special attention to blending the edges until they are completely imperceptible.

# Step by step

This technique is very popular with beginners because it does not need special materials or skills. The result, though, can give life to the most dreary of walls, whatever the chosen style.

Oil-based ragging gives a very distinctive and elegant effect that is in no way boring. It is also a very hard-wearing finish – waterproof, washable, and very resistant to wear – and so is ideal for areas where a lot of wear and tear is expected.

**Materials:**
- *oil-based glaze*
- *burnt sienna*
- *flat brush*
- *cotton rags*

## Tip

The marks left by the rag depend on the fabric used and its thickness. Try doing some ragging using different quality rags, for example fine or loose weave. After experimenting with different types, you can choose the result you like most.

 1

*Dye the oil-based glaze with a bit of artists' oil paint (as described in the section on oil-based painting) and apply it with a brush over a background painted in soft-sheen cream emulsion.*

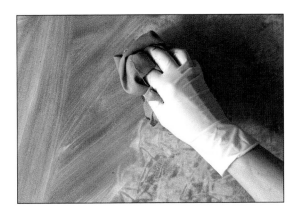

 **2**

*Cover an area of approximately two square meters (20 square feet) with random brush strokes, leaving irregular edges.*

 **3**

*Take a crumpled rag and dab the wet area. It's a good idea to re-bunch the rag in different ways to vary the pattern – this way a characteristic ragging texture is created. Renew the rags when they become soaked. When you have finished this area, apply glaze to the next area. Try to blend the edges well. If you make any mistakes, or you are not completely satisfied with the result, wet a rag with white spirit or solvent…*

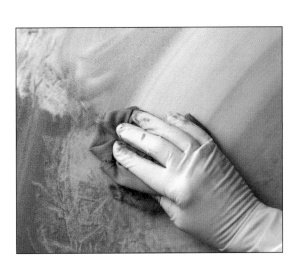

 **4**

*… and wipe the area you want to redo. The slow drying of the oil-based paint gives you more than enough time to rectify any problems.*

# Step by step

# 3. Dragging (water-based)

Water-based dragging is a finish that works with a large range of colors. Because of its delicate and elegant look, it works well in almost any environment. A final wax coat will give it a very pleasant, shiny finish.

**Materials:**
- water-based glaze colored with Ultramarine blue
- cotton rags
- flat brush
- hog-hair softener

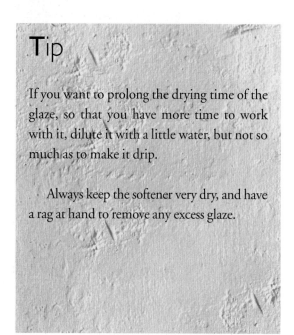

## Tip

If you want to prolong the drying time of the glaze, so that you have more time to work with it, dilute it with a little water, but not so much as to make it drip.

Always keep the softener very dry, and have a rag at hand to remove any excess glaze.

 1

Start with a white wall covered with soft-sheen emulsion paint. Load the flat brush with just enough Ultramarine blue glaze to avoid dripping. Divide the working area in vertical strips about 40 or 50 cm (18") wide, and cover them randomly but making sure the brush strokes are always vertical.

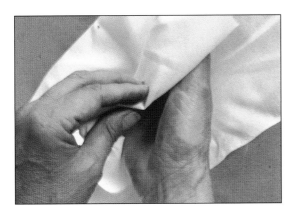

 2

*Immediately after this, take a crumpled rag and drape it over your open hand.*

 3

*Holding the rag this way, slide it with an uninterrupted motion from the top to the bottom of the wall – as if you were scratching the wall. You should get long, slightly irregular vertical stripes.*

 4

*Next, with a dry hog-hair softener, retouch the dragging. Hold the softener firmly by the ferrule and slide it with one continuous movement from the top to the bottom of the wall. Do this as many times as necessary to produce the result you want. If you have a very high wall and have to break the brush stroke in the middle, decrease the pressure on the bristles as you do so, and then you can take up the stroke from where you left off.*

# Step by step ___ 4. Sponging with two colors

This technique allows you to vary both how color is used and the effects it can produce.

As an example, we will look at how to decorate a child's room to give it the look of a green meadow.

**Materials:**
- natural sponges
- water-based glaze dyed in two different shades of green
- acetate strips with wavy edges

## Tip

It's a good idea to limit this effect to certain parts of the wall; apply it no more than a meter or meter and half (3 to 5 feet) in height. This way you will avoid making the children's room look overpowering.

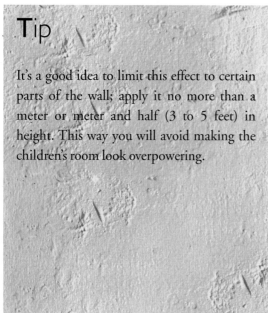

*Mix the ingredients needed to get the water-based glaze, and then color half of it with light dye (or acrylic paint). Use the wet sponge to apply the glaze to the area to be treated.*

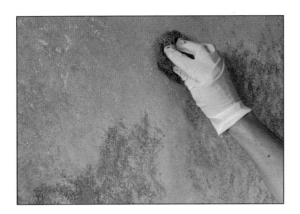

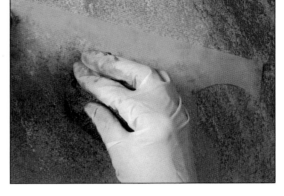

 **2**

Using the darker green, dye the rest of the glaze and apply it over the previous coat in the same way. Where areas of sponging are going to overlap, it's best to apply the lighter color first.

 **3**

Using an acetate cut-out with a wavy edge, put more color over certain areas to suggest hills.

# Step by step

It's quite easy, using say ochre and lemon yellow, to create a striped effect with no relief. This technique requires a special tool: a steel comb that can be found in specialist painting shops; this is used to 'comb' the wet glaze to obtain a narrow striped surface. It is quick to do and suitable for beginners.

**Materials:**
- *flat brush*
- *steel comb*
- *water-based glaze dyed with two different colors. We have used ochre and lemon yellow.*

## Tip

Combing is a very easy technique allowing many variations – you can go for zig-zags, wavy patterns, or even, by combing horizontally and then vertically, grids.

 1

*Alternately brush one color and then the other over a background of cream soft-sheen emulsion. Work in narrow strips that reach the full height of the wall. To get the results illustrated, avoid using colors that contrast very strongly.*

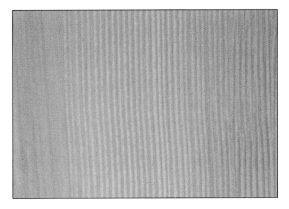

Slide the steel comb from top to bottom to create a striped texture. The pattern produced should be vertical, though as with any hand process, you can expect the lines to fluctuate a little.

To avoid this getting out of hand, you can use a plumb line as a guide.

# Step by step

This unusual finish requires the application of embossing paste. This not only gives a thick texture, which is pleasant to the touch and to the eye, but also helps to cover imperfections.

Colors such as Bordeaux or a rich brown create a sense of great warmth and cosiness.

**Materials:**
- *flat brush*
- *embossing paste*
- *comb with widely separated teeth*
- *water-based glaze made using Bordeaux colored acrylic paint.*

## Tip

It's very important when pulling the comb through the paste that you clean the teeth thoroughly after each application, as they can become clogged. If you don't do this, the result will be not very effective.

 1

*With the flat brush, spread the relief paste onto the surface. Cover a strip of about two square meters (20 square feet), but running the full height of the wall.*

2

The embossing paste should be of a light and elastic consistency; if it isn't, the comb will not produce sharp-defined grooves.

3

Before the paste goes hard, run the comb vertically from the ceiling to the floor. In order to ensure that the lines are vertical, take a door or window frame as reference. Next, apply paste to the strip next to it and proceed in the same way.

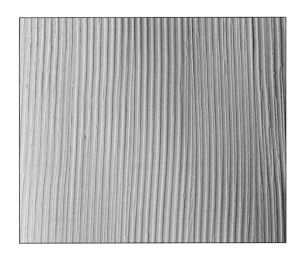

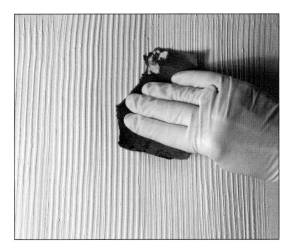

4

Allow the paste to dry completely according to the instructions of the manufacturer. Don't worry if the stripes are a bit wavy – being a hand-finished process, its charm comes precisely from these little irregularities in the finish.

5

Sand down the surface to eliminate imperfections.

# Step by step

 6

*Remove the dust with a brush.*

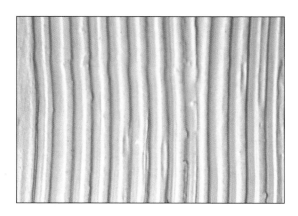

 7

*Apply a coat of latex over the surface to seal it. The latex seals the pores and allows the glaze to spread over the base much more easily.*

 8

*Once the latex is dry, you can apply the Bordeaux glaze with a brush. Work on vertical strips about 50 to 60 cm (2 feet) wide.*

 9

*Remove the excess glaze with a cotton rag, always wiping along (not across) the grooves left by the comb.*

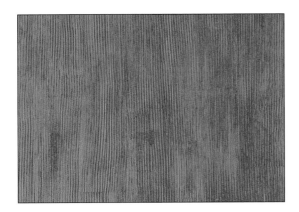

 10

*With relief combing you get a relief surface with a pleasant texture.*

*Earthy colors give a very similar look to that of cardboard wrapping, which can be a cheerful and stylish choice for informal atmospheres.*

*The option of decorating walls by relief combing is very suitable for creating informal atmospheres.*

# Step by step

Stucco, being both classic and subtle, can be used in many different environments.

The finish is extremely resistant to wear and tear, and the washable oil-based glaze makes it ideal for decorating kitchen walls.

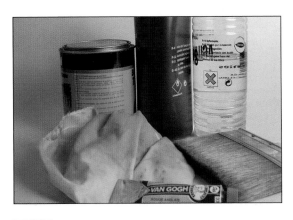

**Materials:**
- *satin varnish*
- *odorless solvent or white spirit*
- *linseed oil and an accelerator*
- *Venetian red artists' oil color*
- *hog-hair softener, rags to clean the softener*

## Tip

Some lighting conditions can accentuate the sheen of the oil finish too much. If this is the case, finish off with a coat of matt varnish to give a softer sheen.

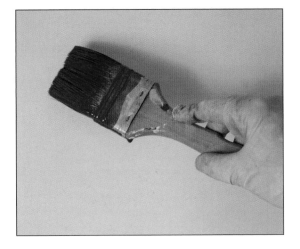

*Prepare the oil-based glaze and apply it with a flat paintbrush over an ochre soft-sheen emulsion.*

 **2**

This application is made using an ordinary paintbrush as all you are doing is spreading glaze over the base.

 **3**

Making brush strokes in all directions, cover an area of approximately two square meters (20 square feet).

 **4**

The following step should be done immediately, before the glaze dries. As this is an oil-based technique, allow sufficient time for treating the wall in areas of approximately two square meters.

 **5**

Holding the hog-hair softener by the ferrule, spread the glaze with random movements to blend the color.

# Step by step

 6

To facilitate blending an area with the one next to it, do not touch the edges of the painted area.

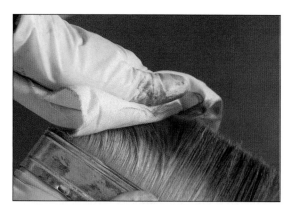

 7

From time to time, wipe the softener to remove the excess glaze.

 8

The hog-hair softener should spread the color without leaving stroke marks.

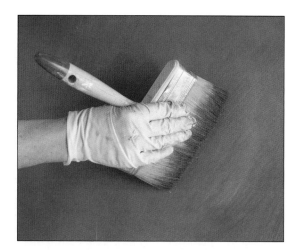

 9

Retouching with the hog-hair softener should gradually smooth the areas of paint, until you get the desired result. Try to achieve a gradual transition from darker to lighter areas.

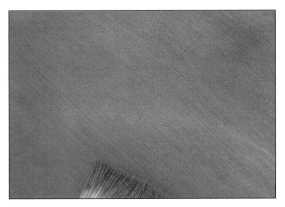

 **10**

Lighter areas are obtained by more persistent brush strokes on the same area, removing a greater amount of glaze.

**11**

This should create a perfect imitation of Venetian stucco.

# Step by step

This oil-based finish is as simple as it is spectacular. Rag rolling on a wall is easy and it's fun; practice first on a thick piece of cardboard if you prefer. The result is what you see here.

**Materials:**
- oil-based glaze
- red ochre in powder pigment form
- cotton rags
- flat brush

## Tip

It is advisable to dye the glaze 24 hours prior to application so that the rag is well impregnated and blends well with the oil-based medium.

If more subtle marks are preferred, use a smaller rag as this will create a thinner cylinder.

 1

Dissolve the red ochre pigment in a small amount of synthetic white spirit and mix it with the uncolored glaze, as described in an earlier chapter.
Although the oil-based glaze goes a long way – you can cover an area of 27.5 square meters (almost 300 square feet) with one liter – make sure you don't run out; prepare enough to cover all of the area you wish to paint and a little more.

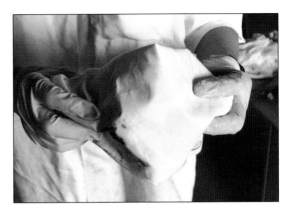

 **2**

Using a flat brush, paint the glaze on to a white, soft-sheen background. Make brush strokes in all directions, covering an area of approximately two square meters (20 square feet). The glaze should have the right consistency, not too thick and not too runny.

 **3**

Next, form a cylinder with a cotton rag.

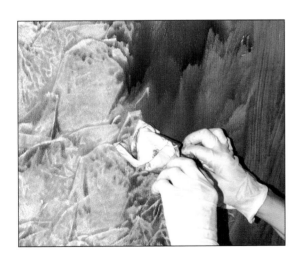

 **4**

Using your fingers, roll it in an up-and-down motion over the damp glaze as if you were using a roller. When there are no gaps left and you are happy with the result, apply the glaze over the next section and follow the same procedure.

# Step by step

# 9. Dragging (oil-based)

Oil-based dragging is rather laborious since it combines two different techniques: stucco and dragging. But it produces a very elegant result that can make the simplest kind of furniture look very smart. Without any doubt, the effort is well worth it.

**Materials:**
- oil-based glaze
- raw amber artists' oil paint
- spirit level
- ruler, pencil, flat brush, hog-hair softener

# Tip

This is a very effective technique when applied to the walls in a narrow corridor (at a height of one or one and a half meters; 3 to 5 feet) since it creates an impression of width. It makes things much easier if you limit the height of the dragging so as to avoid having to use the ladder constantly.

The wall you will be working on must have already been decorated using the stucco technique in the same raw amber shade you are planning to use for the dragging. This is because dragging is applied in thin stripes, leaving the background still visible. See the section on stucco.

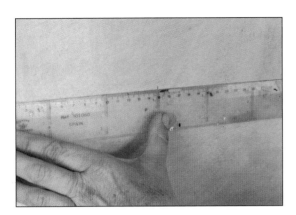

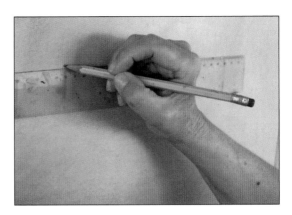

Make marks on the wall leaving 15 cm (6") gaps between them.

As you can see, the base on which these pencil marks will be drawn is oil painted, so there will be no problem erasing them later.

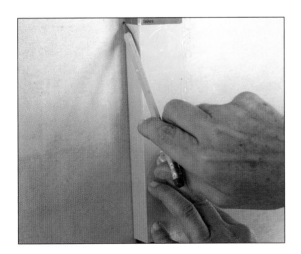

Draw vertical lines using the spirit level.

Stick masking tape along the vertical lines to protect the areas you don't want to paint.

# Step by step

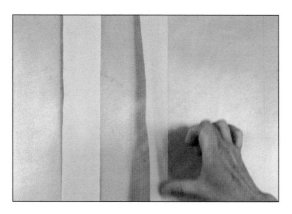

 6

If you suspect that the adhesive on the masking tape is too strong and that you could damage the paint when removing the tape, stick it to another piece of wood (or dampen it with a cloth) first.

 7

Once all the masking tape has been placed on the working area, you can start the dragging. For this technique, the glaze should be thicker than that used for stucco, in other words more varnish should be used.

 8

Apply the glaze with vertical strokes over the first stripe, making sure you don't overload the brush and that you cover the whole area.

 9

Next, slide the dry hog-hair softener vertically down the stripe in one unbroken movement. Repeat the same procedure for the other stripes.

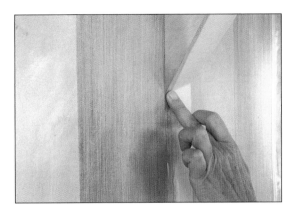

 **10**

*Finally, when the glaze has dried, carefully peel off the masking tape.*

 **11**

*Do so slowly, pulling with one hand and pressing the fingers of your other hand over the area you are pulling it from in order to avoid any damage to the surface underneath.*

# Step by step

This is an easy technique that creates an impression of raffia cloth very realistically. The wall, once painted, can be treated with yellow wax, which would give it the very natural and cosy feel characteristic of wax finishes.

**Materials:**
- pencil over-grainer
- water-based glaze, tinted with natural sienna color

## Tip

To make the effect look more realistic, try applying the technique to only one half of the wall, separating it from the other half with a dado rail running along the whole width of the wall.

Using the pencil over-grainer, apply the glaze to the wall, having previously painted it with a white soft-sheen emulsion paint.

 **2**

*On this, first paint the vertical lines.*

 **3**

*Next, cross those lines by painting horizontally.*

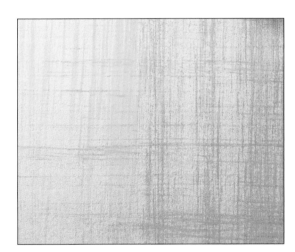

 **4**

*This will suggests a netting effect very similar to the warp of raffia cloth.*

# Step by step

Moiré is a pattern created within certain materials made of thick silk or taffeta, thanks to the easily-molded nature of these fabrics.

With a little practice the typical water-effect of moiré can easily be imitated using a graining rocker.

**Materials:**
- flat brush
- graining rocker
- oil-based glaze, tinted with 'white zinc' artists' oil paint

## Tip

By varying the method, many different results can be achieved, ranging from the subtly elegant to the loud and bright.

Try combining a background and glaze using two complementary colors: the result is really colorful.

Apply the white glaze over a blue-gray background, making vertical stripes about one meter (3 feet) wide.

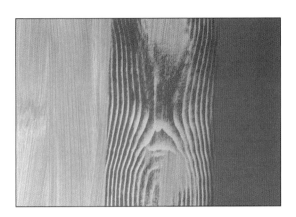

 **2**

Push the graining rocker up and down the surface without stopping, while simultaneously rocking it slightly from side to side.

 **3**

In this way you can create the water-effect of moiré.

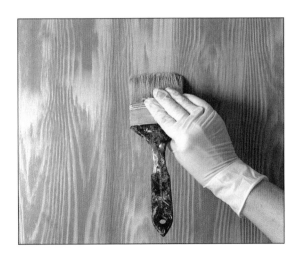

 **4**

To blur the lines left by the graining rocker, slide a flat brush gently over the surface following the vertical lines. Continue this until the lines no longer appear sharp, then follow the same procedure on the next area.

# Step by step

The imitation of wood is a classic decorative paint technique. Recreating pine might seem like a difficult technique, but once you have tried, you'll see how surprisingly easy it is. You can apply it to furniture and any bland-looking surface to achieve a radical change.

**Materials:**
- *ruler, pencil, spirit level*
- *an ochre-colored paint*
- *oil-based glaze dyed with artists' oil color of natural sienna and burnt sienna*
- *graining rocker*
- *two flat brushes*

## Tip

In order to familiarize yourself with using the graining rocker, practice the sliding and rocking motion on a piece of cardboard. Try not to make too many knots as the general effect will seem unrealistic.

Don't be afraid of making a mistake: oil-based paint dries slowly, so you'll have enough time to repeat the procedure until you achieve the result you want.

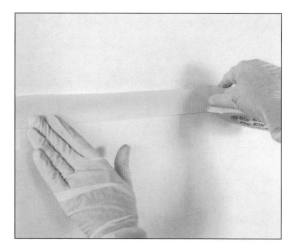

 1

*The wall must already have been painted with a white soft-sheen emulsion paint. On this background, make pencil markings to create horizontal 15cm-wide (6″) stripes. Use a light spirit level to make the job easier. Following these horizontal lines, apply masking tape to define the area to be painted.*

 **2**

This 'plank' background is then painted with the ochre colored soft-sheen emulsion paint, and left to dry. Dye the oil-based glaze with the natural sienna paint, and apply it with fairly random brush strokes.

 **3**

Then, using the burnt sienna, create the slight differences in color characteristic of pine wood. Apply the burnt sienna paint with random brush strokes over different areas of the plank.

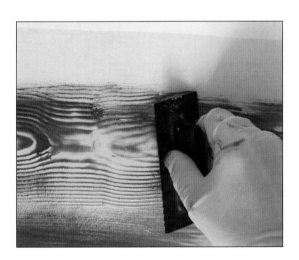

 **4**

Next, create the characteristic grain of pine wood using the graining rocker. Slide the rocker with a firm motion, rocking it slightly as you go, in order to create the appearance of knots in the wood. If the resulting grain is unnaturally sharp, you could soften it with the flat brush, always following the direction of the grain.

# Step by step

This is a very effective technique for decorating the lower half of a wall.

Used with bright colors, like the ones shown here, it can radically change the appearance of a boring corridor.

**Materials:**
- water-based glaze in two colors: golden ochre, and yellow
- sea sponge
- masking tape
- a long level
- graduated ruler, pencil and eraser

# Tip

Larger patterns, like the diamond, will accommodate variations in color – but don't overdo; the result could be far too vivid.

Use similar colors – like blue and green, or yellow and light green – or different shades of one color.

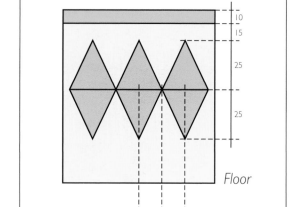

*Floor*

Measure the width of the wall and draw a vertical line dividing it in half. Next, using the level, draw a horizontal line across the wall at the desired height. A second horizontal line, drawn 10 cm (4 in.) underneath the first, creates a band at the top of the area to be decorated. The upper point of the diamond will be 15 cm (6 in.) below this second horizontal. The diamond itself will be 50 cm (20 in.) high by 30 cm (12 in.) wide, as shown in the diagram.

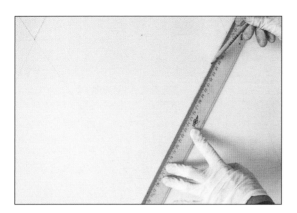

 2

*Draw all the sides of the diamond, using any lines you like for guidance – these will have to be erased later, so don't press on your pencil too hard.*

 3

*Once all the drawing is finished, use masking tape to protect the upper part of the wall, which you don't want to paint, and start sponging the whole area using the yellow paint.*

 4

*Remember that if the masking tape has too strong an adhesive, you can stick it onto some wooden surface or some cloth first to reduce its stickiness.*

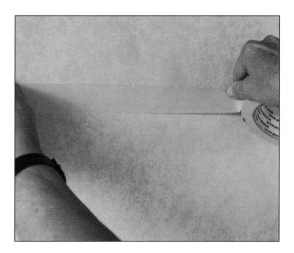

 5

*When the sponging has dried, apply a second glaze, using the golden ochre this time, to paint the diamond and also the upper band. In order to do this, use masking tape along the pencil lines to define all areas that must remain yellow.*

# Step by step

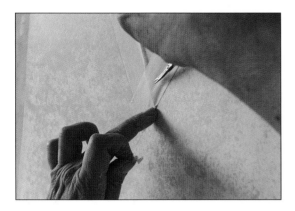

Define the positions of the tips of the diamond very carefully.

Use a sharp cutter to cut the tape that masks the vertex of the diamond. Don't press too hard as you might cut into the wall.

Start to apply the golden ochre glaze with the sponge in the same way as the yellow glaze.

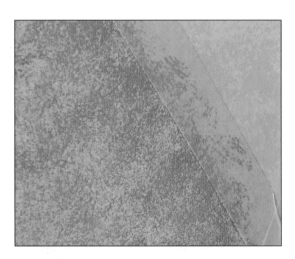

Masking task is invaluable for this type of decoration to avoid spoiling already painted areas. With sponging techniques, as here, clear divisions of color could not be achieved in any other way.

 **10**

*When this glaze is totally dry, carefully remove the masking tape – and admire the final result.*

 **11**

*Here you can appreciate both the sharpness of the lines achieved by using masking tape, and also the harmony between the two chosen shades.*

# Step by step

The appearance of a brick wall can vary a lot depending on its age, the firing of the bricks, and the 'bond' (the arrangement of the bricks).

**Materials:**

- *water-based glaze in: golden ochre, rust red, light gray, and black*
- *stencil paints: burnt amber, white, and black*
- *water-based thinner, sponges, thin brush and stenciling brush, spatter brush*
- *acetate, spirit level, ruler, pencil*

## Tip

Instead of using pieces of acetate as a template, you can define the bricks by sticking masking tape over where the gaps should be.

In this case, though, it is important to use the correct width of tape (about 5mm; 1/4 in.), which can be difficult to find.

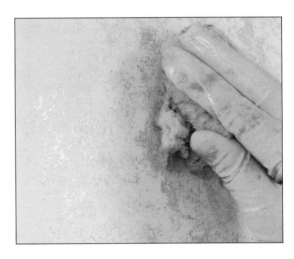

*On an ochre, soft-sheen emulsion paint base, do two lots of sponging: the first one with the ochre paint.*

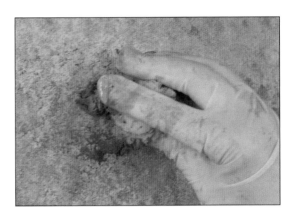

 2

Make sure that you dampen the sponge with water before applying the glaze, and also that you wash it carefully every time you change the color.

 3

On the second sponging, use rust red.

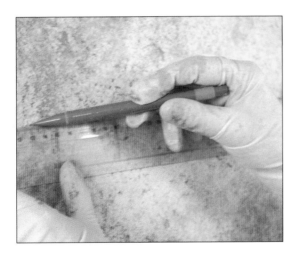

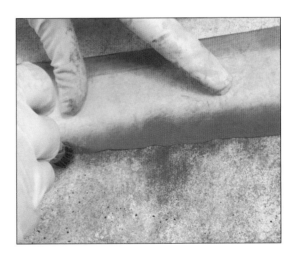

 4

Next, using a pencil draw the lines that will define the bricks. The most common type of bricks are about 25 cm (10″) by 9.5cm (4″) and these are the measurements we will be using. Remember that, just as with any brick wall, the position of the bricks within each row should be out of step with the next one. Use the spirit level to get a perfectly horizontal line.

 5

Place the acetate over the lines. Using the burnt amber, paint in circular motions using the stenciling brush with very little paint on it. This way we will give the bricks a solid, voluminous feel. If you want to create an old brick effect (as in this example), cut the acetate somewhat irregularly.

# Step by step

 6

*Once you have followed this procedure on all of the bricks, apply a light sponging using the light gray glaze.*

 7

*Dilute the gray, black and white paints, and outline the bricks trying to create an impression of relief.*

 8

*Detail of how to create this relief effect.*

 9

*Also, with the diluted black and white paints, draw little cracks if you want to make the wall look very old.*

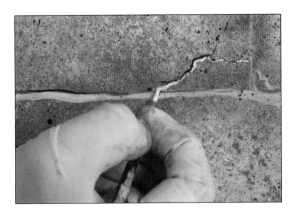

 **10**

*Highlight any small cracks with the white to produce a more authentic effect.*

 **11**

*The porous appearance of old bricks can be achieved by splashing on a little black glaze with the spatter brush. If you don't have one, you could try using a stiff, short-haired brush, or even a toothbrush.*

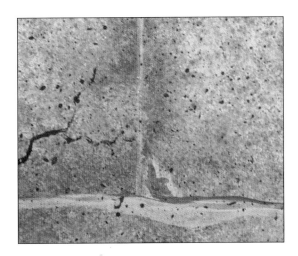

 **12**

*This technique gives a very effective finish for a rustic environment. Brick walls, whether for their warm shade or their traditional material, always give a feeling of cosiness.*

# Step by step

This technique, if properly applied, gives conventional walls a radically different look – of a wall made with stone blocks.

Although the technique is simple, it requires a certain amount of close observation, and so before starting you should carefully examine a few real walls (looking at photographs will do).

**Materials:**
- water-based glaze, tinted in yellow ochre, and a warm light gray, black and white acrylic paint, water-based thinner, sea sponge
- stenciling brush, thin brush, spirit level, ruler, pencil, rubber
- acetate, spray adhesive, absorbent paper

## Tips

If you want to give a stone wall a personal touch, why not try to engrave a bas-relief inscription? For example, Roman numbers, a Latin sentence, etc.

Using diluted black and white paint, and letters of the same size as a pattern, it can be really easy to create this *trompe l'oeil* effect.

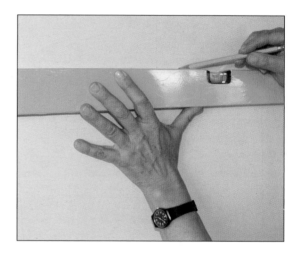

*The wall must be primed with white soft-sheen emulsion paint. It doesn't matter if there are a few irregularities on the surface as the stone we are trying to imitate is not a perfectly flat material. First, using the spirit level, the ruler, and the pencil, draw the rectangles that will become the stone blocks.*

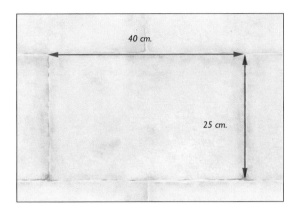

2

Each stone measures about 40 cm (16") by 25 cm (10"). Draw them with the rows staggered, as in a real stone wall.

3

Once all the stone blocks have been drawn, dye some of the water-based glaze with the light gray. You can also use a mixture of white, black, and ochre paints. Never use any dark gray or blue for this procedure.

4

Apply the glaze using a dampened sponge, making sure the glaze doesn't drip.

5

Spread the gray glaze over the whole wall fairly evenly as this will be the predominant color of our old wall.

# Step by step

 6

Over this base, apply a second ochre-colored glaze. In order to impregnate the sponge with color, either dip it in the glaze, or 'paint' its surface with a brush.

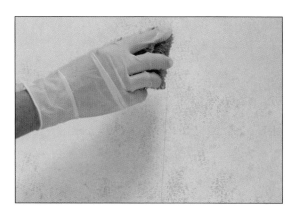

 7

With the latter, the pores remain dry and a more finely doted texture is achieved.

 8

Once the two sponging paints have dried on the wall, you can start drawing the relief and the cracks in the stone blocks using black paint and a stenciling brush.

 9

Cut a piece of acetate with one slightly irregular edge and position it over one of the pencil lines. Dip the stenciling brush in black paint, remove any excess paint with a kitchen paper towel, and apply it to the edges of the stone blocks in a circular motion; this creates shadows.

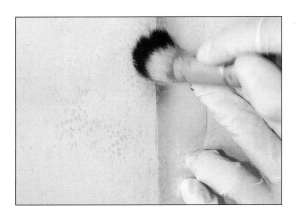

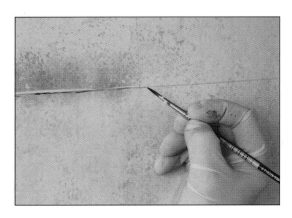

 10

The irregular edge of the acetate will be the one used to define the stone blocks, and at the same time create gaps between the blocks.

 11

The next step is to create the gaps between the stone blocks, and also the natural cracks and irregularities you would expect to see. To do this, lightly dilute some black paint, and use it with a thin brush to paint some irregular lines freehand.

 12

To complete this relief effect, paint a few white lines on the edge of the stones to simulate the effect of sunlight shining on them. These brush strokes must be nearly imperceptible – use a thin brush and lightly diluted white paint. Stonewalls change the feel of a room amazingly, lending it an aura either of antiquity or rusticity.

# Step by step

Gray granite, a rock formed from quartz, feldspar, and mica, is valued in building for its hardness. Following our step-by-step instructions you can create a granite effect very easily. As if by a miracle, you can transform the most unlikely surfaces into solid stone!

**Materials:**
- *natural sponge*
- *oil-based glaze in four different colors. To dye it you will need artists' oil paints in the following colors: raw amber, Paynes gray, ivory black, and zinc white.*

## Tips

If you prefer, try imitating other varieties of this rock, such as pink granite, by using the oil-based glaze of an appropriate color. Either way, the oil base and the final coat of varnish allow this technique to be applied to surfaces that need to be tough and waterproof, e.g. kitchen and bathroom walls.

Finish your work by applying a coat of gloss varnish over the whole surface. The finished result will be very hard-wearing.

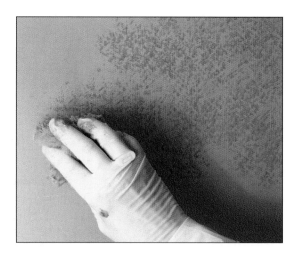

*The wall must be totally smooth and be painted in a blue-gray shade, obtained by mixing white, black, and Ultramarine blue. On this background, apply the first glaze using the sponging technique.*
*The glaze obtained with the raw amber color is a warm medium gray.*

 **2**

Next, apply a second sponging with the anthracite gray glaze, made using Paynes gray.

 **3**

The third sponging is done with black glaze. Apply it more sparsely than before, trying to re-create the look of real granite.

 **4**

Finally, to imitate shiny particles in the rock, carry out the last sponging with white glaze. You could use silver instead, as the essence of this effect is to add small points of great luminosity.

# Step by step

Travertine is a type of chalky stone, light in color, which is known for its veining.

Real travertine is greatly valued in decoration, but with a little skill and some paint you can recreate it very effectively.

**Materials:**
- oil-based glaze without pigment
- Paynes gray, Van Dyck brown, raw amber, brown amber
- flat brush, large feather, white spirit, cloth, badger-hair softener, piece of cardboard

# Tip

You can create the impression of a travertine on a wall.

To do this, draw a few large rectangular areas with a pencil and create 'reserves' of paint with the masking tape, painting each individually. Vein each area at random, vertically or horizontally.

 1

*Spread a clear oil-based glaze on a wall painted with a white vinyl emulsion.*

Put a little oil paint at the end of the flat brush and apply it in vertical strokes over the damp glaze, taking care to alternate the amber, gray, and brown.

Overlap the colors. Don't put too much paint on the brush.

Wipe away excess glaze by rubbing a cloth in vertical strokes. This will give a light scraping effect.

Take a piece of cardboard (cereal boxes are best), and tear it with your hands to give an uneven edge. Drag this edge over the damp paint trying to imitate the natural wave of the travertine. Some of the best results are obtained by using unsophisticated tools!

# Step by step

 **6**

*Move a badger-hair softener over the glaze from side to side.*

 **7**

*This will help to create the soft veining typical of travertine.*

 **8**

*Dipping a bird's feather in white spirit easily reproduces the white stains that are peculiar to this stone.*

 **9**

*Making sure that the feather is not too wet, apply light touches to the wall with the edge of the feather.*

 **10**

*Because white spirit dissolves oil paint, the initial small stain will quickly spread.*

 **11**

*Use the badger-hair softener again to soften these lines, making sure you go across the veining.*

 **12**

*Some tavertines show a lightly spotted effect. This can easily be imitated using a little black paint applied with the side of a feather.*

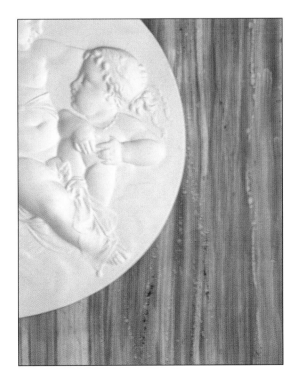

To apply the stamping technique to a wall you should choose a simple design, which will be repeated at regular intervals by the stencil technique.

**Materials:**
- *acetate, stencil brush*
- *orange stenciling paint,*
- *tape measure, pencil and eraser*
- *kitchen paper towels, spray adhesive*

## Tip

The choices are endless… though a simple design is advisable, it does not have to be boring. The design can also be made in two different colors by using two stencils, a procedure that is not very complicated.

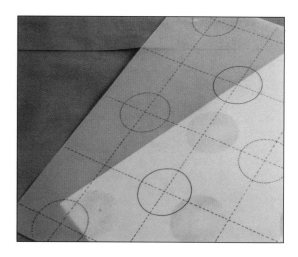

 1

*You'll find it very easy to make your own stencil from a drawing or print you like. Using a photocopier to modify the scale of the drawing if necessary, trace the design using carbon-copy paper onto a sheet of acetate.*

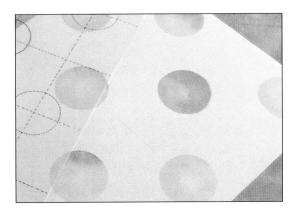

 2

Make sure you know how much space is needed between one design and the next. You should trace more than one design on the stencil and have them set out in the right order.

 3

Make as many reference lines as you need, using broken lines to allow you to reposition the stencil correctly.

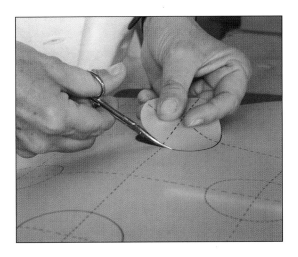

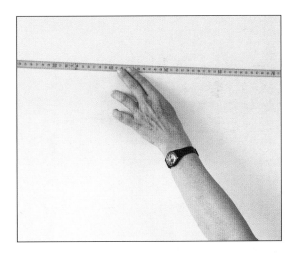

 4

Next, cut out your design. If you do this with a craft knife, make sure you always do the cutting away from yourself, so that you don't lose control and injure yourself. You could use a sharp pair of scissors.

 5

To be able to place the stencils symmetrically, it is necessary to begin stenciling above a central line, which divides the wall in two halves. To do this, measure the wall with a tape measure and mark the center.

# Step by step

 6

Trace the vertical line with the help of a spirit level. Use a pencil and press very lightly (so that it will be easy to erase afterwards).

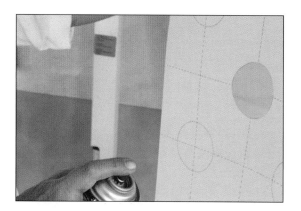

 7

Apply the spray adhesive to the back of the stencil.

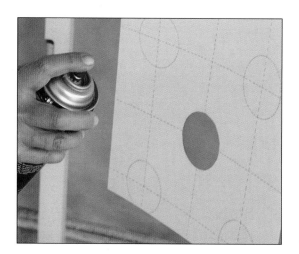

 8

The adhesive spray prevents the stencils from moving and so ensures that the motifs are accurately positioned.

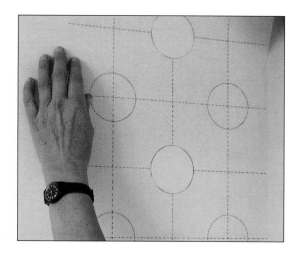

 9

Place the stencil over the pencil line, taking care to place the design at the highest point where you wish to do the stamping.

 **10**

Erase the pencil lines in the space that is going to be painted.

 **11**

Dip the brush in the orange paint…

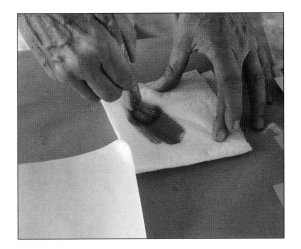

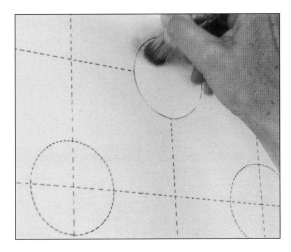

 **12**

…and absorb excess paint on kitchen paper towel. To stencil properly you must make sure that the brush is not too wet.

 **13**

Apply the paint pressing uniformly with the brush and making circular movements. To obtain a relief effect, go over the edges more heavily and cover the rest lightly.

# Step by step

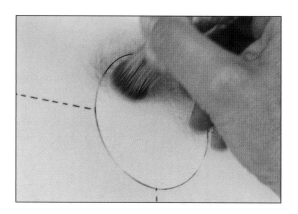

 **14**

*Keep moving the stencil down until you have covered the desired height.*

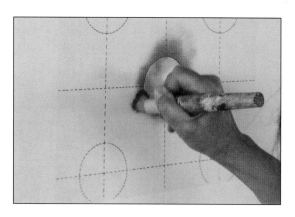

 **15**

*Paint a vertical row of motifs following the line drawn in pencil, always remembering that you must rub it out from the areas that are about to be painted otherwise the outline will look obvious.*

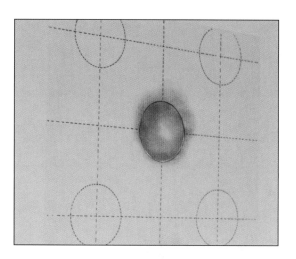

 **16**

*In this diagram you can appreciate how, by means of a greater darkening of the edges, the design acquires relief.*

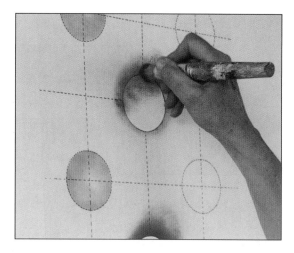

 **17**

*Once you have reached the lower side of the vertical, move the stencil to one side and carry on applying the paint from top to bottom as before.*

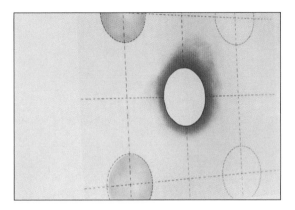

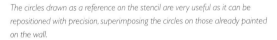

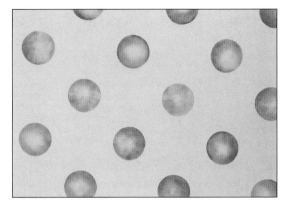

18

The circles drawn as a reference on the stencil are very useful as it can be repositioned with precision, superimposing the circles on those already painted on the wall.

19

It is advisable to check the vertical now and then with the spirit level. A small mistake will become bigger as you go along.

# Step by step

Damask is a mixed technique that combines stamping with stencils over a background prepared by ragging.

This means that you can avoid the rather formal character associated with damask. Small inaccuracies, when repositioning the stencils, will show the craft and skill needed for this procedure and so enhance its attractiveness.

**Materials:**

- *white water-glaze*
- *rust red water-glaze*
- *special brushes to stencil*
- *stencils*

## Tip

When designing your own damask stencils, the best source of information is probably a fabric shop.

Taking a damask print from your own home as an example, you can ensure that the design on the walls matches those on your upholstery and curtains.

*The wall we are using as an example has been decorated with water-based ragging in burnt sienna. See the chapter that deals with water-based ragging.*

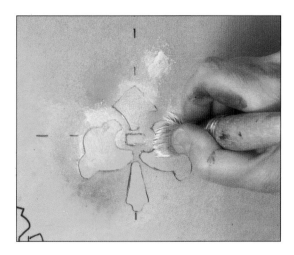

 **2**

Dip the stencil brush in the white glaze. This technique requires the brush to be evenly wet.

 **3**

Absorb the excess paint on a kitchen paper towel; this will spread the glaze evenly and avoid stains.

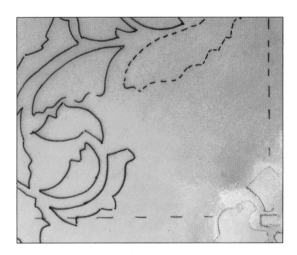

 **4**

To obtain a symmetrical design, begin to stencil at the center of the wall.

 **5**

Start with the design at the highest point of the wall, moving the stencil downwards and to the sides, always aligning the reference lines carefully.

# Step by step

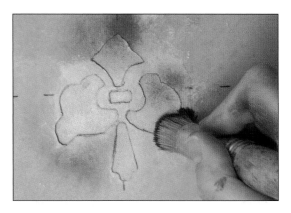

Once the wall is covered in white flowers, reposition the stencil and repeat the process with rust red glaze.

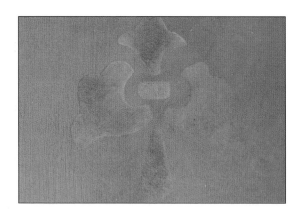

Colors must be applied at random, giving a 'water effect' that reproduces the typical sheen of damask.

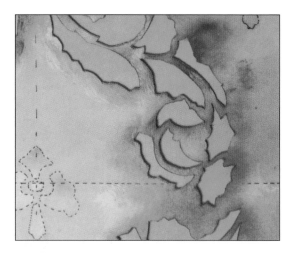

To complete the motif, position the garland stencil, taking as a starting point the flowers drawn with the second stencil.

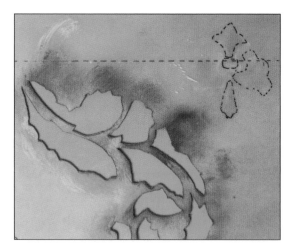

The flower drawn as a reference on the stencil should remain superimposed on what has already been painted on the wall.

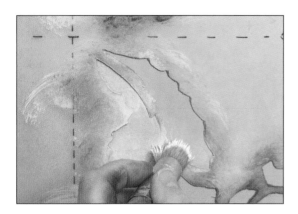

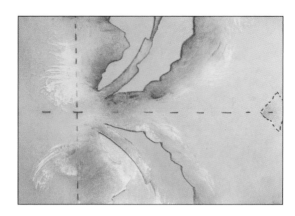

 **10**

Paint with the white glaze first and then with the red glaze, follow the same technique you used for the stenciling of the flowers.

 **11**

When you wish to cover an entire wall with printed drawings, it is essential that the stencil design is done accurately and that all the necessary reference points for correct positioning are indicated with broken lines.

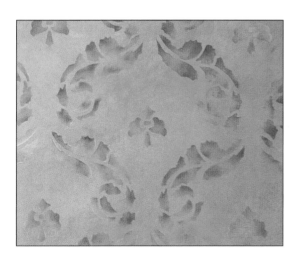

 **12**

It's not difficult to see that this technique was once a humble substitute for wall tapestry. Today it can be considered a very interesting alternative to painted paper.

# Step by step

This finish is achieved with the stencil technique. We will take as an example a popular motif on a tile and create the feel of an Andalusian patio; it can also be applied to a table.

The following instruction will show you how to make a range of stencils and then how to use them to create attractive mosaic designs.

**Materials:**
- acetate, spirit level
- tape measure, ruler, eraser, pencil, stencil brushes
- spray adhesive, ochre, dark green, and black paints to stencil with flat brush, polyurethane varnish

# Tip

If you would like to give the design more of an antique touch, apply a light coat of white glaze before you varnish; it will be better to use a satin varnish rather than a vinyl varnish.

 1

It's very easy to create your own designs from magazines, catalogs, and drawings, or even from nature. As well as having an unlimited source, you will also give a very personal touch to the designs.
Our chosen designs have been copied from a photograph and enlarged with a photocopying machine.

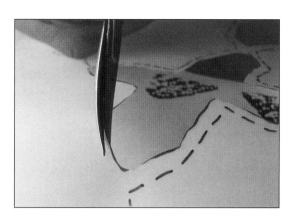

 **2**

*Placing the acetate over the photocopy, trace three stencils: one for the diamond-shaped tiles that outlines the drawing; one for the ochre cross-shaped tiles; and one for the green tiles in the shape of a star. Draw the motifs in a continuous line and the reference points in a broken line.*

 **3**

*Cut out the stencils with a craft knife or a small pair of sharp scissors. The cut-outs of the different tiles must not fit together: this is so as to reproduce the cemented spaces joining the tiles. Cut them a little irregularly to reproduce the effect of a rustic tile.*

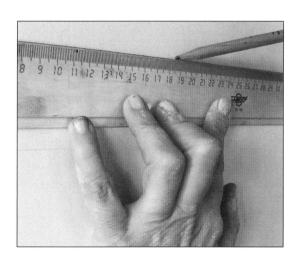

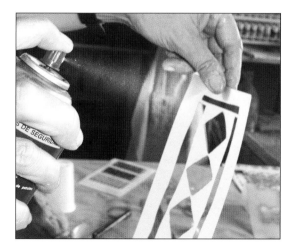

 **4**

*With the help of a ruler and the spirit level, trace a horizontal line on the wall to define where the design will go. In this case, we have painted a plinth halfway up the wall.*

 **5**

*Spray the first stencil, which will form the border, with the adhesive.*

# Step by step

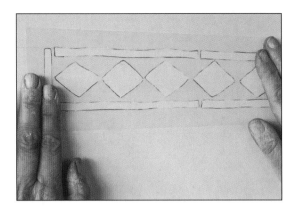

*Place it on a corner…*

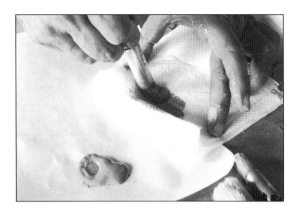

*…and paint the diamond-shaped tiles with the ochre paint, using a circular movement and making sure that the brush is not too wet.*

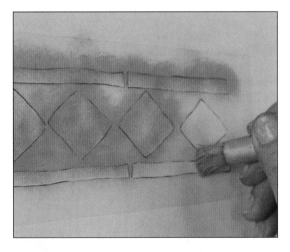

## 8

*Keep moving the stencil along the wall until the defining horizontal line is covered with the border.*

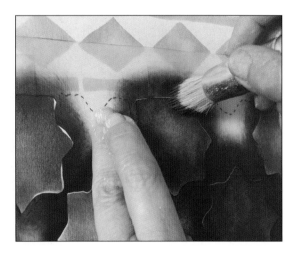

*Next, position the star stencil and paint it green, adding now and then a few drops of black paint to imitate the aged look.*

 **10**

*Finally, stencil the cross motifs with ochre paint, making sure that the broken lines on the acetate coincide with those around the green stars.*

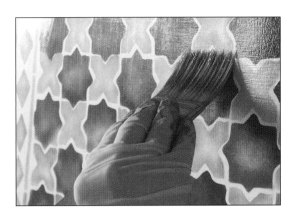

 **11**

*Once the paint has dried, you can apply a coat of polyurethane varnish over the painted area.*

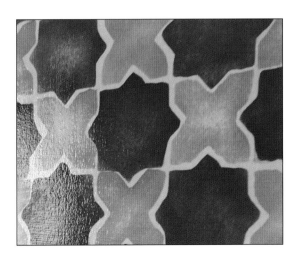

 **12**

*This will make the surface hard, not only protecting it but also giving it the sheen of a real tile.*

# Step by step

It is possible to imitate trelliswork with a climbing plant, quite convincingly, with stencils. You don't need to be a great artist. If you decorate an outside wall with this technique, you must protect it with several coats of matt varnish.

**Materials:**
- brown amber water glaze
- stencil paints in yellow ochre, sky blue, burgundy red, olive green, dark green and brown, acetate, spray adhesive, stencil brushes in different sizes, a very fine brush, kitchen paper towel

## Tip

Get ideas for your design from magazines and catalogs. Keep the cut-outs from the leaf stencils for use later as shields. Where leaves are superimposed cover the front leaves with the shields when stenciling the ones underneath. As you take away the stencil and the shield, you will see that the shield has protected the already painted leaf perfectly.

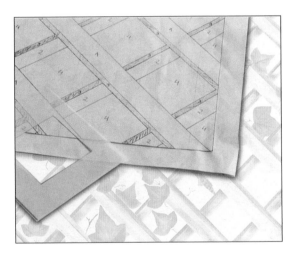

The 'stencil without bridge' technique consists in using several superimposed stencils to obtain a complex design. A correct planning of the areas that have to be cut out will allow you to omit the bridges that otherwise would be visible if you applied the paint to a single stencil. This way you will have a much more realistic effect.
To make up the different stencils that will reproduce the trellis work effect, you must take a model to scale from a drawing of a trellis work.

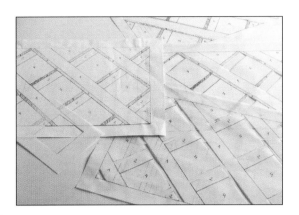

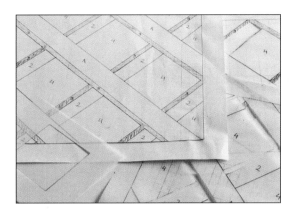

1

2

On a sheet of acetate, trace the complete drawing and cut out the front part of the strips of wood at a 45 degree angle.

The areas that have not been cut out must be marked with broken lines, which will help you to find the correct position of the rest of the stencils. Exactly the same drawing must be traced on a second stencil, from which the front part of

the strips of wood that cross perpendicularly will be cut out, as a second sheet to the one before. The third stencil will be the one that gives depth to the drawing. Finally, on a smaller stencil trace the square formed when the strips of wood cross. It takes some time to make the stencils, but it will make the job of painting the stencils a lot quicker.

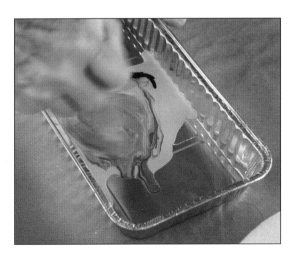

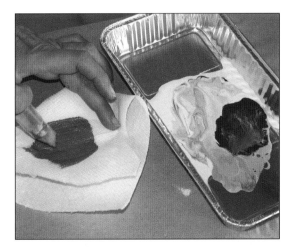

3

Prepare the water glaze with brown amber color.

4

Dip the brush in the water glaze and dry out excess on a kitchen paper towel.

# Step by step

 **5**

*Position the first stencil on the wall and paint the strips of wood following the grain of the wood.*

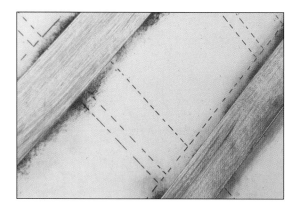

 **6**

*Move the stencil along until you have covered the desired area.*

 **7**

*Next, position the second stencil, and follow the same instruction as for the first one.*

 **8**

*Paint with the same glaze, always following the direction of the wood grain.*

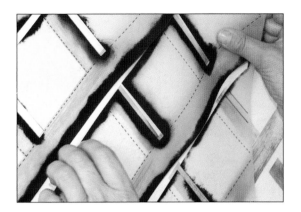

 **9**

*Put in position the third stencil, taking into account the reference lines.*

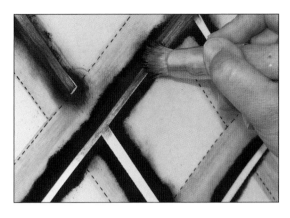

 **10**

*To give the maximum illusion of depth to the drawing, the brown amber water glaze must be a little darker in this area; this effect is obtained by applying more pressure to the brush.*

 **11**

*Once you have applied the paint with all the stencils, the result must resemble the distinctive form of a trellis work. If necessary, you can retouch mistakes made by any movement of the stencils with the help of a piece of acetate.*

 **12**

*The next step is to paint the sky as the background to the trellis work. Use the stencil for the square space between the strips of wood. Apply the blue paint without watering it down; use circular movements and ensure that the brush is not too wet.*

# Step by step

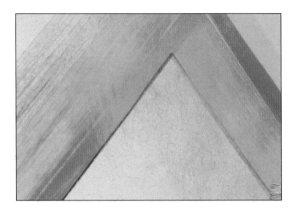

 13

To avoid a flat look, don't apply the paint uniformly.

 14

Finally, taking any climbing plant as a model, such as ivy or vine, cut out a few stencils to reproduce the leaves and stalks. Position them at random on the trelliswork, and then try to replicate the natural way which climbing plants would follow when growing up a trellis.

 15

Apply the olive green paint by tapping the surface with the brush; doing it this way you make sure that the paint covers the background properly, thus avoiding a transparent look on the leaves.

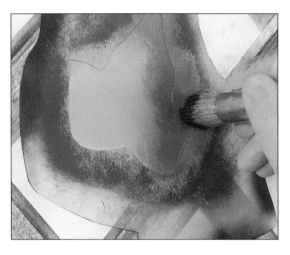

 16

Having the olive green as the background, you can paint in shades of green or burgundy red, according to the plant that you want to imitate.

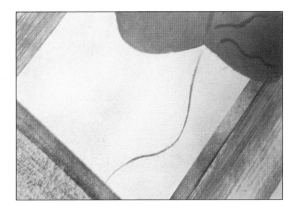

17

The stalks are painted in darker shades, either using a stencil or by free hand.

18

To complete the design, use a fine brush to paint the veins of the leaves in a diluted brown.

# Step by step

The silk-paper technique produces a relief finish that is decorative and that hides imperfections on the surface.

**Materials:**
- *PVA glue, flat brush*
- *a roller, silk paper*
- *brown amber water glaze*
- *antique brown patina*

## Tip

To obtain more texture to the finish, you can crease the silk paper first and then smooth it out before applying to the wall, creating small ridges on the surface.

Although it is often said that the technique will work only on near perfect walls, in fact some of the finishes can be successfully applied to irregular walls.

*Pour into a bowl a sufficient amount of glue to cover the area to be papered.*

 **2**

*With a flat brush apply a coat of PVA glue to the wall.*

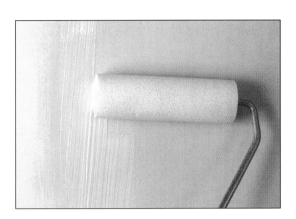

**3**

*Spread the glue uniformly with a roller.*

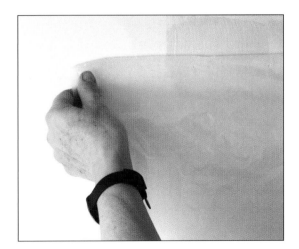

 **4**

*Apply the silk paper sheets, covering the whole surface and overlapping the sides.*

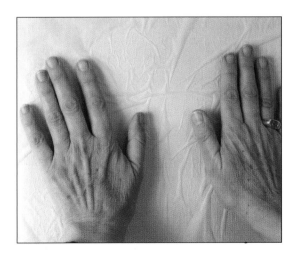

 **5**

*Crease the paper with your hands until you obtain a slight relief all over.*

# Step by step

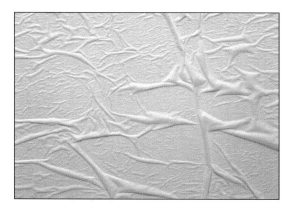

 6

*Let the glue dry as instructed on the bottle.*

 7

*When the glue is totally dry, apply a coat of latex over the whole surface to prevent the glaze from being absorbed by the paper.*

 8

*Apply the brown amber glaze over the dried surface.*

 9

*Cover an area of a square meter (10 square feet) at a time. Water glaze dries very quickly.*

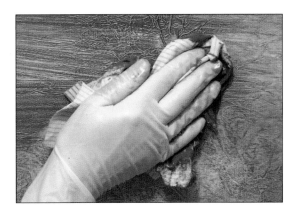

 **10**

*With a cloth, wipe away excess glaze while still wet. This will stress the interesting relief effect formed by the silk paper.*

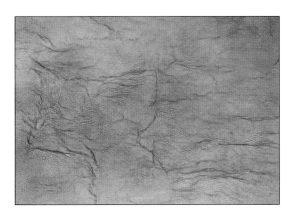

 **11**

*If you finish off this process with an antique brown patina, the surface will acquire an aged look.*

*Exactly the same technique, but in gray color, will look like elephant skin.*

# Step by step

This is a singular technique, which has an original finish and an interesting texture.

**Materials:**
- *craft paper, latex, flat brush*
- *plastic plane*
- *water-based glaze dyed with brown amber and brown sienna*
- *oil-based antique brown patina, cloth*

## Tip

Avoid applying this technique to whole walls. It is better to cover the walls halfway up. If you use glaze in maroon shades you will accomplish a warm finish, similar to leather.

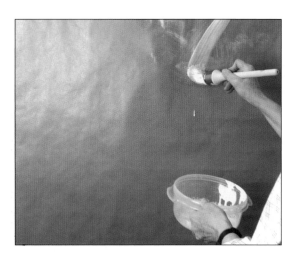

 1

*Lay out the craft paper and paint it with latex.*

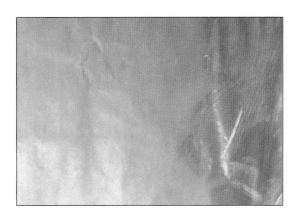

2

You will need the paper to be twice the size of the wall you are going to decorate.

3

Once the latex is dried, tear up the paper into irregular pieces. The size of the pieces is entirely up to you, but avoid large pieces on small surfaces and vice versa.

4

Crease the pieces of paper.

5

Leave them for a while. Once opened, they will present a very striking texture.

# Step by step

 **6**

*Prepare some glaze with a brown amber shade. Follow the instructions given in the chapter on water-based glazes.*

 **7**

*Using the prepared glaze, paint some of the pieces of paper that have been treated with latex.*

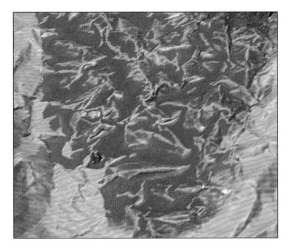

 **8**

*The creases in the paper will be what forms the characteristic relief presented by this technique.*

 **9**

*Prepare a brown sienna color glaze.*

 **10**

*Paint the rest of the pieces of paper in this color.*

 **11**

*The dark brown sienna color blends in perfectly with the dark brown used previously. It is not advisable to use vastly differing tones as the final effect would not be what was required.*

 **12**

*Using an old flat brush apply the PVA glue to the back of a piece of paper.*

 **13**

*Stick it to the wall.*

# Step by step

**14**

*Spread it evenly…*

**15**

*…and go over it with the plastic plane to flatten the surface.*

**16**

*Put on the rest of the pieces of paper in the same way, overlapping the pieces to ensure that the whole surface is covered and alternating the brown and sienna colors.*

**17**

*After you have covered the whole wall, apply a few touches of antique brown patina using a fine brush.*

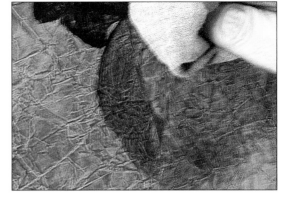

18

*The patina must be spread immediately with a cloth. The ridges on the surface will become darker and will stand out.*

19

*This produces a pleasant antique effect.*

# Step by step

This technique was inspired by the sgraffito used for centuries to ornament pottery and façades.

It is produced by superimposing two coats of paint (or plaster) in contrasting colors and then scraping away the top layer to reveal a design in the first color.

**Materials:**
- *relief paste*
- *plastic trowel*
- *flat brush*
- *pencil with eraser*

## Tip

You can achieve very interesting and bold effects with sgraffito, both through the use of very simple designs and daring combinations of colors.

If you wish larger lines than those made by the pencil, use a thick cardboard to wipe away the relief paste. You can also use a different color as background, but make sure that it contrasts with the color of the outside coat.

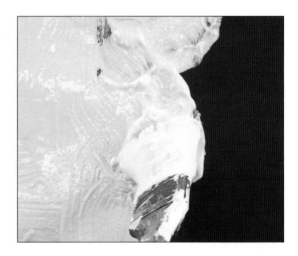

 1

*Apply the relief paste with a flat brush to a wall painted in black. The interest of this design lies in the stark contrast of black and white. But if you prefer, you can color the relief paste with a dye or powdered pigment.*

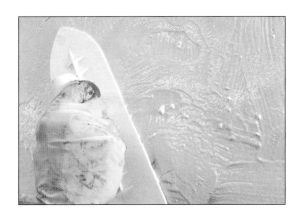

 **2**

Smooth out the relief paste with the plastic trowel while still wet, leaving some lines and irregularities on the surface to simulate a rustic look. The paste has to set a little before you start to draw your design; the setting time will depend on how thick the paste has been applied.

 **3**

With the paste still wet, draw on the surface with the eraser at the end of the pencil.
The drawing must be simple and made out of bold lines, such as the one we propose here.

 **4**

The eraser wipes away the paste, revealing the color applied as background. In this case we have used Oriental calligraphy.

# Step by step

This decorative technique developed when poor families who could not afford pictures used the photographs and prints they had to create an ingenious and effective way of decorating their homes.

**Materials:**
- *photocopies of the chosen designs*
- *white glue, water-based clear varnish*
- *scissors, flat brush, artists' paint brush, antique brown patina*
- *cloth to spread out the patina*

## Tip

Because this technique requires several coats of varnish, the final result is not as delicate as it looks. Part of its charm comes from choosing the right motifs, which can include pictures, antique engravings, post cards, etc. – photocopies of these can also be used.

To obtain a really smooth finish, it is essential to sand the varnish every sixth coat, with wire wool. Do not sand the first few coats as this might damage the images.

 1

*To fix the ink in the images you must apply a coat of clear varnish to the photocopies.*

 **2**

If you prefer a yellow tone, you can apply a coat of lacquer instead of the varnish.

 **3**

Cut out the motifs with scissors. In this case we are using geranium leaves and butterflies.

 **4**

Apply the white glue to the cut-outs and stick them to the wall.

 **5**

This should have previously been painted in satin emulsion.

# Step by step

 6

*Using the plastic plane, smooth out the surface – metal planes can rip the paper easily.*

 7

*Using the artists' brush, apply small quantities of antique brown patina (an alternative is antique glaze).*

 8

*With the help of a cloth spread the patina immediately.*

 9

*Blur the patina in order to obtain a cloudy look, until the whole surface is covered.*

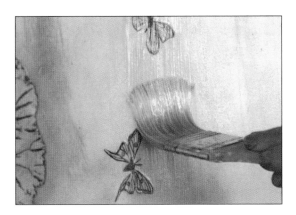

*When the desired effect has been obtained, you can start applying the varnish. It is advisable to apply several coats of varnish, making sure that each coat has dried completely before applying the next.*

*By applying several coats, the thickness of the photocopy will be hardly perceptible.*

# Step by step

With our next technique we propose to imitate the effect of rust on a metal sheet in a very realistic way, with a strong finish – and without the disadvantages of the original.

Ironically, the background to this technique is a wall that has been previously covered with an antirust metal gloss.

**Materials:**
- *furnace black antirust metal gloss*
- *water-base glaze dyed with the following: chocolate brown, rust red, and golden ochre*
- *sponge, flat brush, satin varnish*

## Tip

In this particular finish, a water-based glaze has been applied to a gloss background. This method could cause certain characteristic stains, which would be undesirable in other cases. But in this technique we take advantage of the result and use it to obtain the desired finish. The final look of the wall could even fool experts.

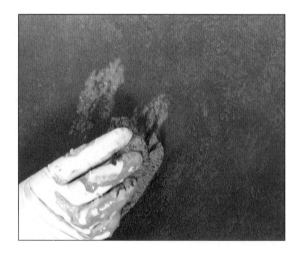

 1

*Mix the brown and ochre colors, and apply with a sponge the first glaze mixture to a wall painted with the furnace black metal.*

126

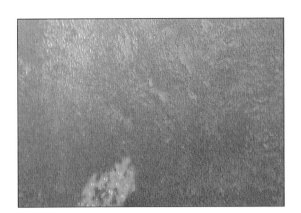

 **2**

*Next, apply a second glaze coat in the chocolate brown color.*

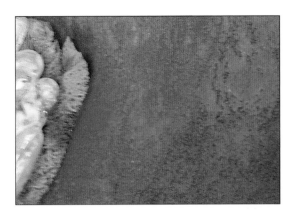

 **3**

*With the sponge, go on to apply the last coat of rust red glaze, taking care to merge the colors.*

 **4**

*You can use the same unwashed sponge since both colors must diffuse together and form blurred areas of color.*

 **5**

*In any rusty surface you can see random stains caused by rain.*

Step by step    127

# Step by step

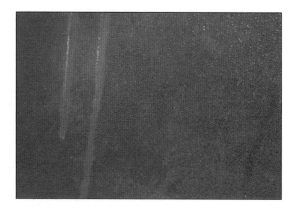

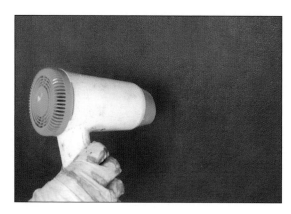

 6

These stains can be reproduced by spraying water over the damp glaze. Quickly, and with the sponge, stop the drops of water from running. It will enhance the different shades of the markings just produced.

 7

You can also use a hair drier to stop the water from dripping. Use a sponge to smooth out the stains.

 8

Always have an example of rusting on hand so that you can create a rusty effect in the most natural way possible.

 9

As with other techniques that imitate various materials, the best results are achieved after studying the texture and chromatic range of various surfaces.

 **10**

*Once you have obtained the desired result, apply a final coat of satin varnish.*

 **11**

*Only through the warm touch of the wall can you determine that the material used is actually not metal.*

# Step by step

This finish has been inspired by the distinctive veining of some stones and will accommodate a wide range of color combinations.

In this example, we have chosen a simple design of white veining against a black background.

**Materials:**

- *black satin gloss*
- *gloss varnish*
- *white water-based glaze*
- *flat brush*
- *a goose feather*

## Tip

The same technique can be used to decorate boxes, trays, or furniture. You must always use goose feathers, which are sold specially to do this kind of finish. Chicken feathers (or those of any other bird) will not produce the same results.

 1

*Prepare the white glaze as usual; pour it into a shallow dish and dip the goose feather into it. To make sure the feather is wet uniformly, you can paint the glaze onto the feather with a brush. The brush can also be used to gather the filaments of the feather in tufts.*

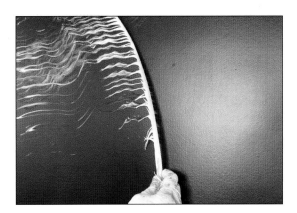

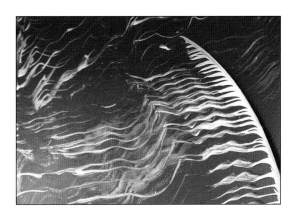

With very little pressure, make wavy lines on the wall using the edge of the feather.

The white lines seem to appear a little transparent to begin with, but once you have varnished the surface they will look darker, so don't overemphasize the colors.

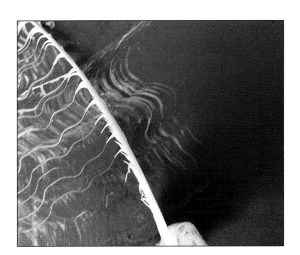

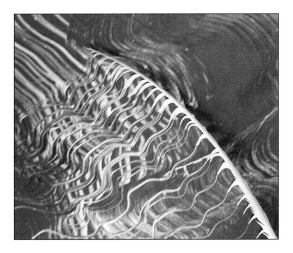

Draw lines criss-crossing with the ones previously drawn, always with wavy movements and overlapping a little.

If you wish to create a whirling effect now and then, apply a little more pressure at certain points.

# Step by step

6

Use the hair drier to speed up the drying of the glaze…

7

…and this way you will control the possible dripping effects.

8

Once the veining of the fantasy stone is finished, let the glaze dry completely.

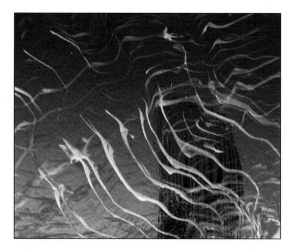

9

Next, apply a coat of gloss varnish all over the surface with strokes in several directions, to make them less visible.

 10

This process can be time consuming, but it is not difficult to achieve.

 11

The finish is elegant and 'eye catching,' and because the varnish makes the finish waterproof, it's ideal for bathroom walls.

# Step by step

This term refers to a wide range of techniques in which a color wash is applied to an irregular background.

The relief, emphasized by the application of color, creates very interesting textures, according to the thickness of the paste applied.

**Materials:**
- *paste for plastering, water-based matt varnish*
- *water-based glaze in red ochre*
- *flat brush*
- *trowel, cotton rag*

## Tip

By accurately controlling the application of the paste, the rustic effect can either be highlighted or made very subtle. As with all finishes that give an irregular relief, it can be an excellent resource for decorating those walls where it would be difficult to achieve the smooth finish needed for other decorative techniques.

 1

*The wall on which you work should be painted in a soft-sheen cream emulsion. Using a flat brush, apply a layer of leveling paste (used for plastering and preparing surfaces prior to painting) onto a pre-prepared base. This paste should not cover the whole of the wall; leave a few gaps at random.*

 **2**

Spread the paste out with a trowel. While spreading, also create some relief, according to taste, by lifting the trowel from the wall from time to time.

 **3**

This movement will form 'crests' on the wet paste that can then be accentuated when the glaze is applied.

 **4**

Allow the paste to dry completely, taking into account the fact that the thicker areas will require a little more time.

 **5**

Once dry, varnish the surface with a matt acrylic varnish.

# Step by step

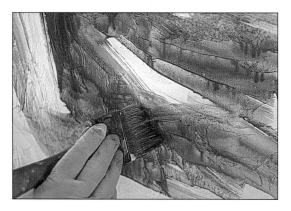

 6

*Once the varnish is totally dry, apply the red ochre varnish with a flat brush.*

 7

*This varnish must be of a fairly liquid consistency, without ever reaching the point of dripping.*

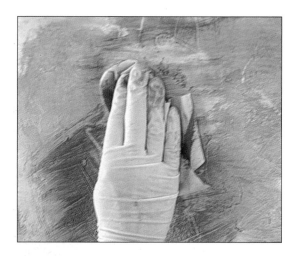

 8

*Using a cotton rag, rub the surface with wet varnish immediately.*

 9

*Working in this way, the varnish spreads and, given the roughness of the base, will be deposited unevenly, resulting in highlighting the relief of the layer of plaster.*

 10

Completely remove the varnish in some of the non-plastered areas in order to allow the cream tone of the base to show through.

 11

In this way, a striking contrast with the red ochre is achieved.

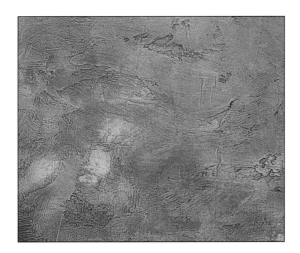

 12

The red ochre, together with the sienna, the white, the indigo or ochre shades, form part of the Mediterranean palette of colors, blending to perfection with the rusticity of this finish.

# Step by step

Both in its dynamic look and in the intensity of color produced by the finishing touches, the dry brush technique lends tremendous visual effect to walls, and greatly simplifies the job of decorating. Few other elements will be required in the room to create an overwhelming effect.

**Materials:**
- white paint, blue acrylic gloss
- water-based glaze, oil-based glaze
- oil paint in dark colors
- acrylic matt varnish

## Tip

'Dirty' tones, such as the blue that we suggest, are really in fashion.

If these shades are agreeable but seem too dark to paint a whole room, apply to one wall only, or to a limited area.

 1

The surface should present a very smooth and soft look. First, give it a uniform finish with acrylic gloss in a dark cobalt blue color.

2

Once the gloss is dry, apply a layer of matt acrylic varnish. This will make the surface smoother so that the glaze to be applied later will spread more easily.

3

The water-based glaze, prepared with white paint, must be applied in small amounts with an almost dry flat brush. Once the flat brush is wet, all the excess must be removed with a rag.

4

Making short and decisive brush strokes in all directions will create a surface full of strength and dynamism.

5

Allow the applied glaze to dry.

# Step by step

 6

Then, with a piece of coarse-grain sandpaper, rub lightly over the whole wall following the direction of the brush strokes, in order to highlight them.

 7

Remove any dust the sandpapering may have produced.

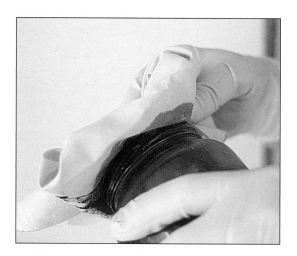

 8

Then prepare an oil-based glaze in a natural dark shade. Apply this glaze with a very clean cotton rag, directly from the pot.

 9

Spread the natural dark glaze over the whole surface, rubbing with a rag.

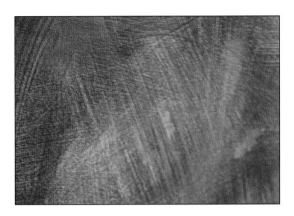

 **10**

Besides modifying the tone and feeling of depth in this way, the final application of oil-based glaze will also give a soft-sheen look typical of an oil finish.

 **11**

The final result shows that wall painting often does not differ too greatly from artistic painting.

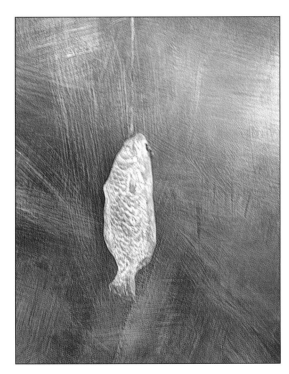

 **12**

The impact of this finish can be particularly highlighted when combined with contemporary furnishings, or if it forms part of a minimalist decor.

# Step by step

Natural stone is a building material that is now practically banished from our dwellings. Precisely because stone was used in ancient castles and lordly estates, interiors decorated in stone have the quiet medieval air of these buildings about them.

This technique produces a rough wall with a warm appearance, which is very much in keeping with country houses.

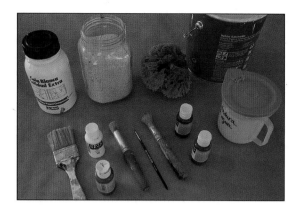

**Materials:**
- *white emulsion, fine light-colored sand, glue*
- *water-based glaze*
- *acrylic paints in dark green, black and white shades*
- *flat brush, sponge, stenciling brushes, a fine brush for drawing outlines*

## Tip

Try this technique with three-dimensional objects, such as large urns, flowerpot stands, or ornamental garden objects, including inexpensive plastic objects. They will be completely transformed.

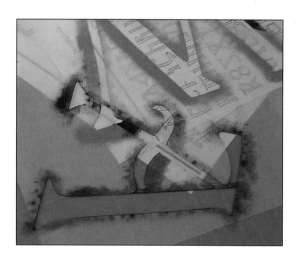

 1

*We have highlighted the medieval character of this finish with a stencil design, which in this case imitates some letters engraved on the stone, although any other motif such as Celtic knots or geometric reliefs would have been equally effective.*

**2**

For this stencil you will need:
- acetate
- enlarged photocopies of the original you want to reproduce
- felt tip pen
- scissors or craft knife

**3**

First, mix the sand with the white emulsion and the glue. The final consistency of such a mix must be fairly thick so that it does not drip, nor separate from the sand once dry.

**4**

Apply a thick layer of this mix to the wall using a flat brush. Given that this preparation is thick and covers well, it will conceal any small irregularity or crack there may be on the wall.

**5**

Next, while the surface is drying, prepare four water-based glazes in the usual way with the four above-mentioned acrylic colors.

# Step by step

 6

*When the base is completely dry, apply the dark glaze using the sponging technique.*

 7

*Then, still using the sponge, apply light touches of green glaze. This color will enhance the old look of the wall.*

 8

*To accentuate the porous look of the stone, use soft sponging with the black glaze. Always keep in mind the appearance of authentic stone and try, where possible, to copy from real examples.*

 9

*Lastly, sponging with a white tone will create the characteristic relief surface of the stone.*

 **10**

The next step involves engraving an inscription on the imitation stone. For this, instead of a hammer and chisel, we revert to the stencils we made!

 **11**

The stenciling is done in dark tones with acrylic paint, using a round stenciling brush. Always remove excess paint from the brush on a piece of rag or kitchen paper before painting the motifs.

 **12**

With a fine brush, and in the same tone as the painting, outline the letter to accentuate the impression of relief.

# Step by step

As with all decorative techniques using gilding, this technique produces a warm and sumptuous finish, with some hues that evoke what is without a doubt man's most precious metal throughout history. Compared with other much more complex and costly techniques, such as the application of gold leaf, this technique is equally spectacular while being much more affordable.

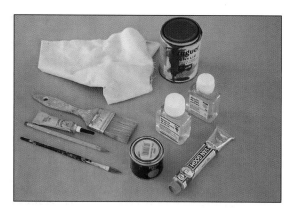

**Materials:**
- *rust red gloss, golden yellow gloss, oil-based glaze*
- *a natural dark shade of paint, and a tube of gold embossing paint*
- *flat brush, the bristle cut at an angle*
- *sandpaper*

## Tip

The gilding technique does not have to be bound to a classic and complicated decorating style. It can be used with a certain amount of irony, on the least suspecting surfaces (such as bathroom walls, for instance) or combined with extremely simple pieces of furniture, in order to obtain amusing and lighthearted décors.

 1

*To create the garlands to adorn the paper, you'll need:*
- *. paper*
- *carbon paper*
- *pencil*
- *photocopies of the original motif*

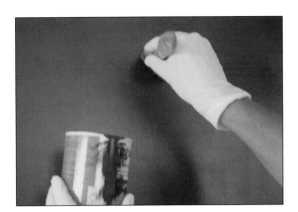

**2**

First, paint the base with rust red gloss. The surface should be perfectly smooth and without defects.

**3**

Prepare an oil-based glaze, as explained in the relevant section of this book, mixing linseed oil, turpentine, and gold-yellow gloss.

**4**

Apply this glaze to the red base, painting in vertical lines. The light consistency of the glaze forms lines through which the background color can be glimpsed.

**5**

Allow the gold glaze to dry completely.

# Step by step

 6

Next, rub lightly with coarse-grained sandpaper to highlight the grooves drawn on the wall…

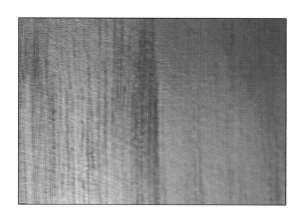

 7

…following the brush stroke, until you achieve the required effect.

 8

At this moment, the gold wall has a slightly and somewhat irregular lined effect.

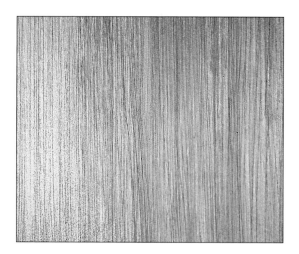

 9

This type of finish could also be used on picture frames and small items of furniture.

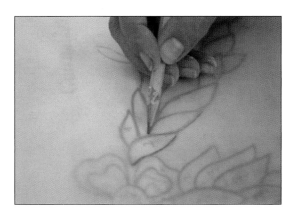

 **10**

*In this particular case, adorn the gold wall with a garland in the same tone.*

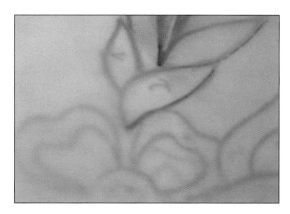

 **11**

*For this, trace onto a sheet of paper the drawing already obtained by photocopying an original to the appropriate scale.*

 **12**

*With a sheet of carbon paper, transfer this drawing onto the wall, going over the lines with a pencil…*

 **13**

*…and exerting sufficient pressure to make the marks from the carbon paper visible.*

# Step by step

 14

The most elaborate drawings can be transferred onto the wall using carbon paper…

 15

…without a talent for drawing and with the assurance that the proportions will not be altered.

 16

Once the drawing of the garland has been completely transferred, go over the traced lines with embossing paint.

 17

This paint is very easy to use as it comes in an applicator tube.

**18**

Lastly, darken the leaves and the flowers of the garland with natural dark glaze using a brush with bristles cut at an angle. Given that the surround offers a slight relief, it will be easy to prevent this filling going over the edges.

Walls decorated in gold tones reflect light in a very warm and sensual way. If you like candlelight, and a hint of an opulent room, don't hesitate to put this decorative technique into practice.

If you like candlelight and sumptuous neo-boroque atmospheres, try out this decorative technique.

# Step by step

On walls that are old, whitewashed, and subject to wear, the layer of whitewash gradually becomes finer, until it eventually disappears in some areas, leaving the stone or brick on which it has been applied exposed. With this technique you can recreate this effect without having to wait years!

**Materials:**
- *rust red soft-sheen emulsion*
- *white matt paint*
- *alcohol*
- *flat brush, rag*

## Tip

The finishes that artificially age furniture or walls, as in this case, are highly fashionable as they remove the coldness from contemporary environments. For this reason, this type of process combines perfectly with decorative elements of ultramodern design and cold materials, such as metal and glass.

 1

**Additional materials:**
- *stencil*
- *rust red acrylic paint*
- *two stenciling brushes*
- *roll of kitchen paper*

 **2**

*A simple stencil decoration will give this wall a country feel.*

 **3**

*First, prepare the surface with a layer of rust red soft-sheen emulsion.*

 **4**

*Allow the paint to dry completely before applying white paint on top.*

 **5**

*It is very important to apply the white paint in thin layers with the flat brush only lightly covered with paint. Therefore, once the brush has been dipped with paint, always wipe off the excess on the inside of the tin or on a wooden board.*

# Step by step

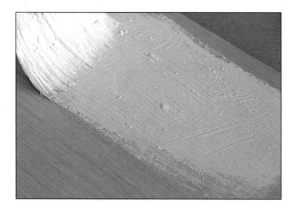

 **6**

*In this way, as well as being dried of excess, the paint is distributed evenly between the bristles of the flat brush.*

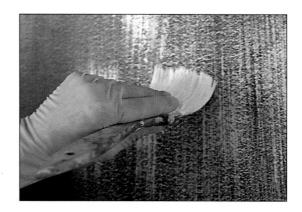

 **7**

*Begin by painting with vertical brush strokes, with the flat brush always very dry.*

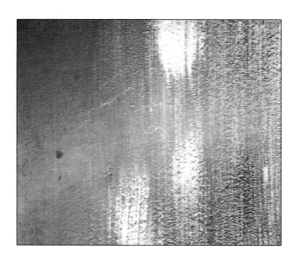

 **8**

*The rust red of the base should remain almost covered with white matt paint.*

 **9**

*From time to time, make a perpendicular line, crossing over previous brush strokes, to spread the paint more effectively and to create a more casual effect.*

 **10**

*Cover the whole wall in this way and leave the paint to dry.*

 **11**

*The next step involves removing or rubbing out part of the white matt paint with which you will have almost hidden the rust red. With a cotton rag and a little ethyl alcohol, rub the areas where you want the color of the base to appear.*

 **12**

*Neither the form nor the size of these areas should be regular.*

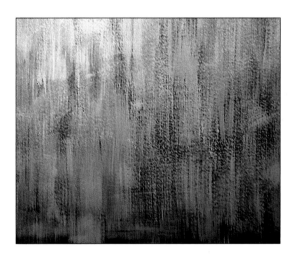

 **13**

*If the appearance of the patches looks too artificial, or you want to make corrections, you can always paint over them again with the white matt paint...*

# Step by step

**14**

...keeping the flat brush almost dry, until you achieve a more natural look. This process may be repeated as many times as necessary.

**15**

Once you are satisfied with the appearance of the wall, you can then proceed with the stencil decorating. Place the stencil in the appropriate place and paint the motif on the wall with the rust red acrylic paint.

**16**

It's a good idea to choose a simple motif, the same color as the base.

**17**

Next, with the same rust red paint, draw and touch up the design.

 18

Lastly, rub lightly with sandpaper, both the stenciling and the rest of the wall, if necessary, to highlight the old appearance that this finish conveys.

 19

This is the appearance of the wall when decorated with this technique. The end result is comparable to that obtained when stripping furniture, as you can see the traces left on the surfaces by the passage of time (and by successive attempts at decoration).

# Step by step

# 33. Chalk glaze

Chalk is one of the most popular materials used in southern Europe to paint façades. Its whiteness, dazzling in the southern sun, is what gives great charm to Spanish, Italian, and Greek houses. However, due to its low cost and its high quality finish, it is also a very attractive technique for interior decoration. In the following example, we have dyed chalk with one of the colors with which it seems to have an especial affinity: blue.

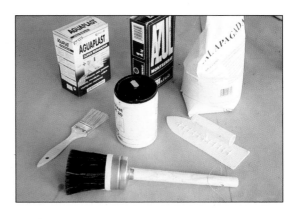

**Materials:**
- *chalk, latex, blue color*
- *leveling paste*
- *plastic trowel*
- *paintbrush and flat brush*

## Tip

The color of this glaze greatly diminishes in intensity when dry. It is therefore quite difficult to predict what the final tone will be. So it's a good idea to have wooden boards or cardboard available on which to test the color.

 1

*The end result obtained with this technique will depend to a great extent on the characteristics of the base on which it is being applied. A smooth wall will give rise to a finer surface, with a feel similar to an eggshell, whereas…*

**2**

...a rough or irregular wall will create a rustic finish, characteristic of the old houses. If the walls are too smooth for your liking, it can easily be imitated using the following method:

**3**

Dilute the leveling paste in water, dissolving all the lumps that form, until an elastic consistency is achieved.

**4**

The paste must not be so thin that it drips, but should be liquid enough for you to be able to spread it easily with a flat brush.

**5**

Recoat the wall with this preparation, avoid applying very thick layers, as these crack easily when the paste dries.

# Step by step

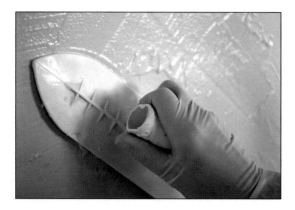

 6

*Spread the leveling paste with the plastic trowel. The rounded angles of this tool make it difficult to scratch the surface, a real danger when using metal trowels.*

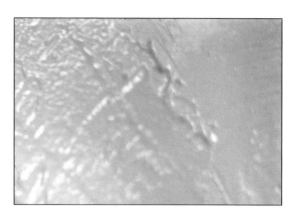

 7

*While spreading the paste, create the required degree of relief.*

 8

*By lifting the trowel from the wall, you can create a relief similar to crests or small undulations.*

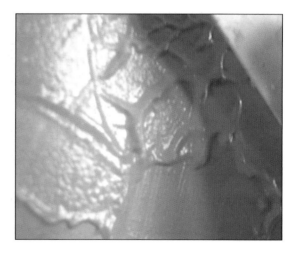

 9

*Don't be afraid to experiment: on wet paste you can always make any modifications you consider necessary until the desired result is acquired.*

 **10**

To prepare the chalk glaze, mix approximately 2 parts of water, 1 of latex, and 1 part of chalk.

 **11**

Next add the blue powder and whisk the mixture a little.

 **12**

The traditional (and best) way to apply paint to the chalk is with a very thick paintbrush.

 **13**

Given that the base is rather porous and that it is advisable to coat it generously, this paintbrush allows you to load the necessary amount of glaze without having to wet it every few minutes.

# Step by step

 **14**

*In very little time a large surface will be coated in color.*

 **15**

*Don't worry too much if at first the brushstrokes are very obvious.*

 **16**

*While the chalk glaze is still wet, the blue will appear much more intense than anticipated…*

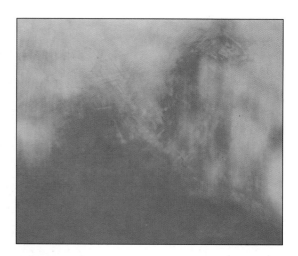

 **17**

*…but as the water evaporates the color will become less saturated.*

 **18**

*Gradually, the wall will begin to acquire the sky-blue tone envisaged.*

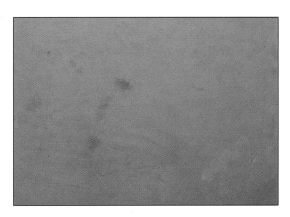

 **19**

*Chalk glaze has the irresistible charm of simplicity. It is one of the quickest and most economical techniques described in this book, though it produces a surface that has a certain fragility and can flake. For this reason, it is not advisable to use in rooms where it will face a good deal of wear and tear.*

# 4. Glossary

# 4. Glossary

## A

### Accelerator:

Any substance that will shorten the drying time of a paint. Oil paints, for example, normally take over a week to dry, a time that can be greatly reduced by an accelerator.

### Animal-based glue:

Any binder obtained by boiling the bones or hide of animals, frequently used in painting before synthetic products were sold commercially. One of the finest glues is obtained from rabbit skin.

## B

### Base coat:

In most decorative paint techniques it is the first coat of paint. It forms the foundation of the technique, the glazes being applied over the base coat. Base coats are either water-based or oil-based. The best base coat for a water-based glaze is satin emulsion. The best base coat for an oil-based glaze is either emulsion or gloss.

### Binder:

Any adhesive substance that binds pigments together, for example gum Arabic in watercolor blocks.

### Blurring:

The toning down or softening of the edges of an area of color or a mark.

### Border:

(Also called a frieze) an ornamental feature consisting of a motif repeated in a line, as on the edges of carpets or fabrics, or along a wall.

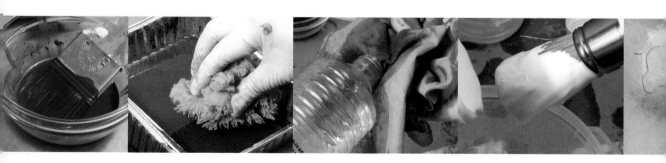

# C

## Casein:

A water-soluble protein obtained from milk, used for centuries as a natural binder in paints. Not in use any more because of its short life.

## Color:

In terms of home decorating, it is important to remember that colors are affected (a) by the other colors around them, and (b) by the kind and intensity of the light that falls on them, natural or artificial.

## Color theory:

Color theory is a set of established relationships between colors. The color spectrum is divided into 3 levels of color and placed in equal parts around a color wheel. The first level consists of the primary colors: yellow, magenta (red), and cyan (blue). These are the so-called pure colors because they are obtained without mixing. Between the primary colors are the secondary colors, obtained when 2 primary colors are mixed equally: orange (magenta+yellow), green (yellow+cyan), and violet (cyan+magenta). The third level of colors are the tertiary colors, resulting from a mix of a primary color and an adjacent secondary color in equal amounts: purple (magenta+violet), or turquoise (cyan+green). Opposite colors on the color wheel are called complementary.

## Combing:

The use of a specialist steel tool to 'comb' the wet glaze in order to achieve a narrow striped surface. Relief combing requires the application of embossing paste to create a thick texture.

# D

## Découpage:

A decorative technique in which coats of clear varnish (or lacquer) are applied to photocopies of motifs and designs.

## Dispersion:

The diffusion of pigment in a paint (water-based or oil-based). The minute particles that form the pigment are not dissolved chemically (as salt is in water) but spread out uniformly and are held in suspension.

## Dragging:

Dragging is a technique that can be achieved using water- or oil-based paints. After the wall has been painted, a rag is dragged across the surface to achieve an irregular, vertically striped effect.

## Dye:

Any coloring substance. Dyes are classified according to their origin: mineral, vegetable, animal-based, or synthetic (which were not in use until the 19th century).

# E

## Emulsion:

A compound of two liquids that do not dissolve into one another: one of the liquids is dispersed through the other in minute drops.

## Emulsion paint:

A water-based paint. Commonly used to paint walls and ceilings, it is economic, odorless, and easy to use. It can be bought in a wide range of colors or can easily be dyed with coloring agents.

# F

## Filler:

A hard-drying paste used to fill holes or cracks; it hardens on contact with the air. It is sold in powder form or ready prepared in tubes and tins.

## Finish:

The appearance of a painted surface in terms of the way it reflects light. There are three levels:

### Gloss
When light is reflected brightly.

### Matt
When reflected light is diffused and dull.

### Satin
When the effect lies between the above two.

## Fitch:

A hog-hair paint brush particularly suitable for painting with oils. In decorative art it can be used for free-hand marbling.

## Flogging:

A decorative technique that involves striking a wet glaze with a brush in order to make the glaze spread out in circles, allowing the base color to come through.

## Fresco painting:

A decorative technique in which paint is applied to wet plaster. As the plaster dries, the color becomes chemically bonded to it, making the image permanent.

# G

## Glaze:

A semitransparent paint, lightly dyed, that is applied over a base coat. Many decorative paint techniques are based on the way the glaze is treated – smeared, dabbed, flogged, etc. A glaze can be water-based or oil-based.

## Gloss paint:

An oil-based paint that has a waterproof finish. Gloss is widely used to cover surfaces that need to be durable and have to be cleaned often. It usually contains resin of melanin and can be used as a background to oil-based glaze.

## Gouache:

A watercolor paint to which white has been added to make it opaque.

## Granite:

A dark gray stone that because of its strength is widely used for building. It is composed of quartz, feldspar, and mica.

# L

## Latex:

Water-based binder used in paints. Made of water, resins, and other substances, it has the consistency of a thin emulsion.

## Level:

A tool used in carpentry and other crafts to achieve a straight and level line. It is usually made of steel or other sturdy metal and contains a bubble in the center with colored liquid. When a line is uneven the bubble tilts to one side.

## Light:

In choosing a color scheme for a room it has to be remembered that colors are affected by: (a) whether the light is natural or artificial; (b) the light's intensity; (c) its direction and evenness. Also, the chosen finish will determine how the light is reflected.

## Linseed oil:

Produced from linen seed, linseed oil is one of the most widely used solvents in oil painting. A drying oil, it reacts with the oxygen in the air to produce a hard film in which the color pigments are trapped. Linseed oil forms a hard and washable surface.

## M

## Marble:

A limestone, widely used in architecture and sculpture, that often has veins or markings in different colors according to its variety. Different types of marble often take the name from the place of origin, for example Egyptian green. The look of marble can be accurately reproduced by marbling techniques.

## Moiré:

Watered silk; the appearance of watered silk recreated by decorative paint techniques.

## O

## Oil painting:

A painting technique in which pigments are mixed with a drying oil, usually linseed oil. Oil paints dry very slowly, and so may have to be used with an accelerator. They are sold in tubes in an extensive range of colors and can be used to dye oil-based glaze.

# P

## Palette knife:

A tool rather like a knife with a thin and very flexible blade used to apply filler. Can be metal or plastic.

## Pigment:

The coloring substance used in a paint or glaze.

## Plaster:

To cover walls with mortar or fine plaster to achieve a smooth surface suitable for painting. A plastered wall must be sealed before being painted.

## Plumb line:

A tool for testing whether a line is vertical. It consists of a length of string to which a cone-shaped piece of metal has been attached.

## Primer:

A first coat of paint or sealer to prevent porous surfaces from absorbing too much paint.

# R

## Raffia:

The realistic impression of the warp of raffia cloth can be achieved by painting several thin lines vertically, and then painting over them horizontally.

## Ragging:

A decorative technique that involves dabbing a wet glaze with pads of crumpled cloth. The effect depends on the type of cloth used (e.g. fine or coarse weave) and on how the surface is dabbed.

## Resin:

A sticky substance obtained from pine and fir trees, used as a binder in paints; now largely replaced by synthetic substitutes.

## Retardant:

Any substance, such as glycerine or resin, that will lengthen the drying of paints so as to allow more time for a technique to be carried out.

# S

## Sandpaper:

Special paper which, being covered on one side with fine very hard particles, is used to smooth down surfaces. It can be used to prepare a surface for painting by removing unevennesses or roughness; or to make varnish extra smooth. The size of the particles will determine the finish.

## Sgraffito:

A decorative technique that involves scratching through a top layer of paint or plaster to reveal a different colored surface beneath.

## Solvent:

(Or paint thinner). Any substance that can dissolve the organic or inorganic substances found in binders, usually used to clean brushes. An example is white spirit, which is used with oil-based paints.

## Sponging:

A decorative technique in which natural sea sponges are used to apply water-based glaze to a wall. It creates a very distinctive texture. Artificial sponges are far less effective.

## Stencil:

A decorative technique in which a motif is created by dabbing paint over a design that has been cut out of a sheet of paper or plastic. Stenciling is particularly useful with motifs that have to be repeated.

## Stucco:

Wall covering made of a lime paste and marble powder; it is often cast or worked into shapes. Usually white, it can be dyed. Stucco itself is a technique that is the preserve of professionals, but the stucco effect can be created quite easily.

## T

## Texture:

The appearance of a surface, whether smooth or rough; its tactile quality.

## Thinner:

Colorless substance used to give paint the desired painting consistency – either to make it easier to apply or to create specific effects.

## Trelliswork:

A lattice of light wooden or metal bars used as an ornamental feature or as a support for climbing plants. They frequently form diamond shapes.

## Trompe l'oeil:

(From the French *trompe l'oeil*, a "deception of the eye".) A painting that creates a strikingly life-like, three-dimensional image.

## Turpentine:

A volatile oil obtained from conifers and used as a solvent in oil painting. When painting interior walls, it is better to use odorless synthetic products.

# V

## Varnish:

A clear, colorless paint applied as a final coat to protect a painted surface. The most widely used varnishes are made of a solution of resin combined with oil and are available in different finishes: gloss, matt, and satin. These varnishes can be colored using small amounts of oil paints or universal stainers.

## Veining:

A decorative technique that imitates the veins found in marble. This effect is easily reproduced with brushes, feathers, or special tools.

# W

## Watercolor:

Painting technique in which pigments are dissolved in water. Because watercolors are not opaque, they are applied in thin translucent washes. They come in two forms: as a dry block made up of pigment bound with gum Arabic, and as a concentrated paste in small tubes.

## Wax:

Wax can be used as an alternative to varnish for finishing surfaces. The application of wax produces a matt finish that acquires a soft sheen when rubbed with a cloth.

```
747.94        Pujol-Xicoy, Reyes
Puj
        Decorative wall painting
             for beginners

1-03-47                      14.95
```

**LYONS DEPOT LIBRARY**
**P.O. Box 49**
**Fifth and Broadway**
**Lyons, CO 80540**
**(303) 823-5165**